World of Hummingbirds

Erik Hanson

Photographs by Tony Mercieca
Illustrations by Amelia Hansen

STACKPOLE BOOKS

Published by
STACKPOLE BOOKS
5067 Ritter Road
Mechanicsburg, PA 17055
www.stackpolebooks.com

Printed in China

10 9 8 7 6 5 4 3 2 1

First edition

Cover design by Tessa J. Sweigert
Berylline hummingbird photo on page 113 © M. Grosselet/VIREO

Library of Congress Cataloging-in-Publication Data
Hanson, Erik A.
    World of hummingbirds / Erik Hanson; photographs by Tony Mercieca; illustrations by Amelia Hansen.—1st ed.
        p. cm.
    Includes bibliographical references and index.
    ISBN-13: 978-0-8117-3606-0 (alk. paper)
    ISBN-10: 0-8117-3606-7 (alk. paper)
    1. Hummingbirds. I. Title.

QL696.A558H36 2009
598.7'64—dc22

2008052656

Contents

Introduction

Hummingbirds radically challenge some of the traditional images that people might have of birds. Hummingbird wings move the way insect wings move, and people who see hummingbirds frequently in parts of the United States sometimes think they *are* large insects. Members of many species prefer to have feeding territories, but even hummingbirds that cannot maintain territories are consistently aggressive. Some less tactful scientists have used words like "hostile" and "belligerent" to describe them. It is clear that hummingbirds are intense and beautiful, quite intelligent, and seldom casual in their approaches to any task.

In general, the flights and bodies of hummingbirds are characterized by a variety of extremes and apparent contradictions. They spend between 55 and 75 percent of the day perching, but many of them tend to perch for only a few minutes at a time. Thus, most people observing hummingbirds would say they are always "on the go." A hummingbird may have more than 1,600 individual flowers in its territory and appear to be greedy at first glance, but the amount of superfluous nectar in the territory may actually be fairly small. And the heart rate of a hummingbird can be up to twelve times higher at one time during a day as it is at another time. The heart of a flying hummingbird may beat at more than 1,200 beats per minute. When the same hummingbird enters torpor, a kind of metabolic conservation mode that slows all bodily functions, its heart may beat only a little more than 100 times per minute.

Hummingbirds only live in North America, Central America, and South America. Sixteen species of hummingbirds enter parts of the United States and Canada to breed, usually during the spring and summer. More species live and breed in Mexico, and Mexico is technically part of North America. But the discussion of "North American" species is meant, in this book, to refer to the species that breed in the United States. There are approximately 328 species of hummingbirds in the world, and most of these species live close to the equator in Central America and South America. Scientists cannot always tell if one group of hummingbirds should really be viewed as a distinct species, so the true number of species tends to not be exact.

With so many species living in Central and South America, it is not surprising that hummingbirds have influenced the mythology of people living in these areas over the last few thousand years. A myth describing "the origin of honey," taken from the oral literature of the Kaingang and Shokleng peoples of Brazil, has been translated a number of times. In this myth, a toucan and a woodpecker are trying to get honey from a beehive. The toucan finds the hive, the woodpecker pierces it, and the two birds eat the honey. A hummingbird tries to get some of the honey, but the two other birds refuse to share. In response, the hummingbird hides water from the other birds and lies about his knowledge of the whereabouts of the water. In one ending to the myth, the hummingbird is—and by extension all future hummingbirds are—punished for lying and made to feed on only small amounts of water, from nectar, at a time. As one researcher noted, because hummingbirds are always looking for nectar, they are also, in a sense, always looking for water.

This myth gives insight into hummingbird behavior. It is true that hummingbirds tend to take in "small" amounts of water at a time from small amounts of nectar. But many hummingbirds get an enormous amount of water, sometimes 1.6 times the weights of their bodies, from their daily nectar intakes. Additionally, many hummingbirds follow woodpeckers around and eat tree sap from holes that the woodpeckers have drilled. Although tree sap is a very important food for several North American species of hummingbirds, especially at certain times of the year, honey is actually harmful to hummingbirds and can kill them. In their territoriality and opportunistic consumption of tree sap, hummingbirds could, with reference to the myth, be viewed as being self-interested.

In other mythology, hummingbirds are associated with the bravery and power of warriors or hunters. The Aztec people of Mexico described Huitzilopochtli (which loosely translates as "hummingbird associated with the left" or "hummingbird associated with the South") as a man who became the "God of Sun and War." Hummingbirds are not birds of prey and do not hunt, but they nonetheless move in ways that are decisive and precise and reminiscent of the movements of warriors.

People have also viewed hummingbirds in the context of light, and the power of light, in other mythology. Some of the myths of the Aztec people have included stories of warriors dying and essentially taking hold of the sun, beginning in the East, making it rise to its highest point, and then turning into

Colorful and exotically plumed hummingbirds, such as the streamertail, Jamaica's national bird, have inspired countless myths and folktales.

hummingbirds. Another major hummingbird myth comes from the Kekchi Mayan and Mopan Mayan peoples who lived in parts of Mexico and Central America, people whose descendants now live in parts of Belize. In this myth, there is a hunter who represents the sun at night and whose name has been translated as "Young Jaguar Sun" or as the juvenile "Hidden Sun." He is weakened early in the story, much as the sun, hidden behind the earth at night, is thereby weakened. He then puts on the exterior and feathers of a hummingbird and, appearing as a hummingbird, goes to court a woman. The woman is representative of the moon. The father of the woman kills the hummingbird, but the hummingbird comes back to life as the hunter and ultimately persuades the woman to go away with him.

The "Hidden Sun" therefore uses the feathers of a hummingbird to brighten himself as part of his strategy to regain power and rise again in the morning. The myth is thought to be a kind of explanation for the way the sun sets, interacts or negotiates with the moon, and then rises again and ceases to be hidden. In this myth and in Aztec mythology, hummingbirds are, again, associated with both the movement of sunlight and with bravery or power in the face of death. The view of hummingbirds as being brave has some validity, given that hummingbirds migrate alone and that many ruby-throated hummingbirds migrate annually across the Gulf of Mexico, alone, in a single flight.

Hummingbirds are, in fact, able to capture and transfer light in remarkable ways. One feature of the iridescent colors of hummingbird feathers is that the color is only visible from certain angles and can, in this sense, be like a hidden or elusive brightness. The scientific names of rufous, broad-tailed, and Allen's hummingbirds all include the word *Selasphorus*, which means "light-carrying." Parts of the scientific names of calliope, blue-throated, lucifer, and magnificent hummingbirds have also been derived from words that have to do with light, such as the Latin or Greek words for "shining" or "radiant."

This book describes the physical and behavioral characteristics of North American hummingbirds. Hummingbirds use a variety of complex strategies to set up and patrol feeding territories and interact with other hummingbirds. This book also includes a field guide to the sixteen species that breed in the United States and a discussion of the breeding and courtship behaviors, migration, and anatomy of hummingbirds. Finally, there is a discussion of strategies to use when you are setting up a feeder, photographing hummingbirds, and watching hummingbirds in the wild.

1

What Makes a Hummingbird?

FLYING MACHINES

Hummingbirds, with their extreme wing movements and flight maneuvers, present scientists and bird-watchers with various contradictions. On the one hand, hummingbirds can fly and perform in ways that seem durable and powerful. In this sense, a hummingbird is like an elite athlete among birds and at an evolutionary pinnacle of adaptations for flight. On the other hand, aspects of hummingbird flight are exquisitely sensitive to changes in air temperature and atmospheric pressure. In this sense, hummingbirds are fragile and delicate organisms that depend on a precise set of conditions for optimal movement and health.

Hummingbirds are very tiny birds. Hummingbirds weigh between 0.07 and 0.7 ounce and are generally about 2 to 8 inches long, measured from the tip of the bill to the end of the tail. To put the mass of a hummingbird into perspective, it is helpful to note that the U.S. quarter and nickel coins weigh, respectively, approximately 0.20 ounce and 0.17 ounce.

Most of the species living in North America are from 3 to 5.5 inches long and weigh between 0.11 and 0.32 ounce. These species include the smaller rufous and black-chinned hummingbirds, which weigh between 0.11 and 0.14 ounce and are about 3 to 4 inches long, and the larger species of magnificent and blue-throated hummingbirds, which weigh between 0.25 and 0.32 ounce and are about 5 to 5.5 inches long. The Cuban bee hummingbirds, which are generally the smallest, weigh just over 0.07 ounce and are about 2 inches long. Giant hummingbirds are the largest hummingbirds and live in South America. These birds can be 8 or 9 inches long and weigh up to 0.71 ounce.

Despite their small sizes, hummingbirds display extraordinary feats of muscular performance. Although hummingbirds do not appear to have much weight to carry in flight, their muscles are very powerful on a per-unit-mass basis. A number of aspects of the flight and physiology of hummingbirds help to explain this power.

The giant hummingbird, the world's largest, lives in western South America. The smallest, the tiny bee hummingbird, lives in Cuba.

Unique Wing Structure

The wing structures and capacity for hovering flight make hummingbirds similar to insects and unique among birds. The joints of the wrists and elbows of hummingbirds do not flex during flight. All of the wing motion originates at the birds' shoulders. A hummingbird can, through its shoulder movements, vary the angles at which its wings are rotated, either tilted forward or backward, and the distance with which its wings beat above and below its body.

Even though the wing motions occur at the shoulder joints of hummingbirds, the bones of a hummingbird's hands make up most of the length of the skeletal portion of the wings. A hummingbird's upper arm, between the shoulder and the elbow joints, and the forearm, between the elbow and the wrist, are more or less always in a V shape, with the elbow joint bent. When a hummingbird is facing forward with its wing extended out to the side, the point of the V is pointing toward the tail of the bird. The hand extends out from one of the two ends of the V, and the tip of the hand extends to about half of the way down the hummingbird's wing. The other half of the wing, from the tip of the hand to the tip of the wing, consists of the outermost primary feathers. The primary feathers are those whose tips extend from the parts of the wing tissues that surround the hands.

Analyzing Flight

It is helpful to note some of the variables that can be used to analyze hummingbird flight:

- The wing beat, which is an upstroke and downstroke of the wings.
- The wing-beat amplitude, also referred to as the wing-stroke amplitude or the flap angle. This is the angle of the wing at the upstroke, in relation to the plane of the bird's body, plus the angle of the wing at the downstroke. The wing-beat amplitude of a hovering hummingbird may be between 160 and 180 degrees.
- The wing-beat frequency, which is the number of wing beats per second. This variable is sometimes expressed in hertz (Hz), which are cycles per second. A 60 Hz wing-beat frequency would be 60 wing beats per second.
- The wing rotation about the shoulder joint.
- The horizontal flight speed, expressed in miles per hour (mph).

The wing-beat amplitude provides a numerical value for the degree of up-and-down motion of hummingbird wings, and this is probably most easy to imagine in the context of hovering. When an ordinary bird is landing, it makes intuitive sense that the bird will tend to flap its wings farther upward and downward, to sort of hover for a second or two before landing. A hummingbird will hover for sustained periods of time by moving its wings through an almost complete 180-degree motion.

It is important to note that wing movements can be described in relation to either the ground or in relation to the relatively straight line that is defined by the hummingbird's back and body. When a hummingbird is flying forward at its greatest speed, which tends to be roughly 26 mph, the bird's body is roughly parallel to the ground. During this type of flight, the wings tend to move the most upward and downward, in relation to the ground. When a hummingbird is hovering, the line of the hummingbird's back tends to be angled upward at a roughly 45-degree angle, much as a person could lean forward from the waist and produce a 45-degree angle with his or her back.

When hovering, hummingbirds generally hold their bodies up and down, or at a 45-degree angle, while beating their wings horizontally—parallel to the ground—as illustrated by this male broad-billed hummingbird.

During hovering flight, however, the wings tend to move along an axis that is actually horizontal and parallel to the ground. Thus, hummingbirds generally tend to move their wings "up and down" with respect to the lines of their bodies. But because they tilt their bodies forward during hovering flight, the wing movements of this flight are with respect to the ground actually forward and backward. Even though the backward flight of hummingbirds involves fairly complex wing movements, this general concept still applies. The wings, during backward flight, are at roughly 90 degrees in relation to the line of the hummingbird's back at each "upstroke" and "downstroke." But during backward flight, the hummingbird's body is oriented vertically to the ground.

The maximal wing-beat amplitude of nearly 180 degrees is simply the sum of the 90 degrees of positive upstroke plus the 90 degrees of negative

1   2   3   4

downstroke. If you straighten your arms and point them to the sky, then bring them down to your hips, you've accomplished the same 180-degree range of motion. It is important to note, however, that it is not really possible for human arms to approximate hummingbird wing movements. As discussed above, the 90 degrees describe the angle between the line of the wing and the line of the hummingbird's back. The 90 degrees do not refer to the angle between the line of the wing and the line or plane of the ground.

The flight speeds of hummingbirds are not as high as one might expect, given the capacity of a hummingbird to rapidly arrive at and disappear from a feeder. The horizontal flight speeds of hummingbirds, measured in laboratory wind tunnels or elsewhere, range from 18 to 32 mph and tend to average

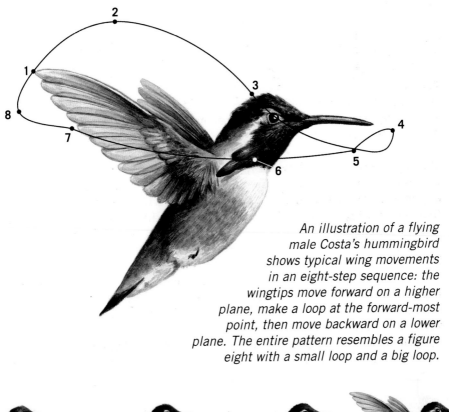

An illustration of a flying male Costa's hummingbird shows typical wing movements in an eight-step sequence: the wingtips move forward on a higher plane, make a loop at the forward-most point, then move backward on a lower plane. The entire pattern resembles a figure eight with a small loop and a big loop.

about 26 mph. A hummingbird may dive, such as to attract a mate or defend its territory, at speeds of up to 60 or 80 mph.

The wing-beat frequency of a hummingbird tends to be in the range of 25 to 44 Hz, frequencies that are lower than those of many insects. Hummingbirds may at times display wing-beat frequencies as high as 70 Hz, but the frequencies tend to be consistently in the range of 25 to 44 Hz. These frequencies are comparable to the roughly 30 Hz frequency of the hawk moth. In contrast, honeybees exhibit wing-beat frequencies between 230 and 240 Hz, flies beat their wings at roughly 200 Hz, and midges may demonstrate frequencies as high as 1,000 Hz.

Great Maneuverability

The rotation of the wings around the shoulder joints helps hummingbirds to fly in different directions and change the directions of their flight. For example, hummingbirds can fly backward by rotating their wings up to 180 degrees. Hummingbirds that are flying backward also position their bodies vertically, so their tails are pointing toward the ground. During backward flight, hummingbirds also shorten the "downstroke," which in this case is not a downward movement but a forward movement. The key point is that during the "upstroke"—or "backstroke" of backward flight—the wings rotate essentially 180 degrees. This is not the same 180 degrees that is the maximal wing-beat amplitude. As a result of the rotation during backward flight, the tops of the wings face toward the ground. A similar rotation would occur if a person held his or her arms out with the palms up and then rotated the elbow joints to make his or her palms face down.

The wing movements of backward flight can be envisioned as the natural extension of the movements of a bird that is about to land on a perch. An ordinary bird may hover like this for a second or two before perching, and the wings of the bird essentially produce backward thrust that slows the bird down. In backward flight, this slowing down of forward movement is extended into sustained, reverse flight. The wing rotation during backward flight causes the end of the wing to move in a kind of circular whirlwind, almost like the arm of a person treading water.

Fuel for Flight

Hummingbird physiology also seems to have become adapted for the use of large amounts of oxygen and carbohydrates. Scientists cannot say that hummingbirds "like" nectar *because* it may maximize their metabolic efficiency, but the simple sugars in nectar do rapidly improve the birds' muscular performance.

Scientists found, for example, that sugars improved hummingbirds' muscular efficiency within a period as short as thirty minutes. After hummingbirds had been fasted, scientists reintroduced the birds to a source of

Flight Adaptations Among Mountain-dwelling Hummingbirds

Different populations of hummingbirds also display adaptations, in flight parameters, to different environmental conditions. Scientists have found, for example, that hummingbirds living at high altitudes tend to be larger and have larger wings in relation to their body masses. This evidently helps to compensate for the aerodynamic conditions at higher elevations, conditions that include a reduction in the density of the air and a lower concentration of oxygen in the atmosphere.

Hummingbirds living in locations such as the Andes Mountains, at elevations of over 11,023 feet, have larger wings but also increase their wing-beat amplitudes in flight. This means they move their wings farther up and farther down with each stroke so that the angle between the upstroke and downstroke may be as high as 180 degrees. Interestingly, the wing-beat frequency does not appear to change, either up or down, in hummingbirds living at higher elevations. Additionally, the wing-beat frequency also tends to be lower in larger hummingbirds and higher in smaller hummingbirds. Thus, to compensate for a larger body size, larger hummingbirds tend to take larger wing strokes, particularly at high elevations, but not more wing beats per second. There is an extreme precision with which the flight parameters of hummingbirds must vary in order to fit into an environment.

Researchers found that hummingbirds living in valleys were only able to outperform high-altitude hummingbirds in short-term feats of flight. For example, the high-altitude birds were at a disadvantage when it came to rapidly accelerating upward or forward, such as would be required to catch insects or impress a potential female mate. Hummingbirds tend to be remarkably aggressive and will also dive or fly rapidly to keep other birds away from nectar-rich flowers. Larger bodies and wing strokes allow high-altitude hummingbirds to hover just as efficiently as their low-altitude, valley-dwelling counterparts.

simple carbohydrates, or sugars. Hummingbirds would have access to these simple sugars from plant-derived nectar in the wild or, less commonly, from hummingbird feeders. As the birds utilized the sugars and relied less heavily on fats, they were able to use between 16 and 18 percent less oxygen to produce the same amount of chemical energy and the same muscular power output. This means that simple sugars from nectar are a preferred or, as scientists noted, a "premium" fuel for muscular performance in humming-birds, especially under the lower-oxygen conditions at high altitudes.

Because hummingbirds are able to efficiently adapt their flight to changes in environmental conditions, scientists must look at very specific environmental factors that may influence hummingbird flight. At high altitudes, for example, the air contains oxygen, nitrogen, and other gases and is less dense than it is at lower altitudes. Air that is less dense provides less aerodynamic lift and provides essentially less mass for the birds to "push" down against and lift themselves up with. This decrease in lift also makes it more difficult for planes to take off at high altitudes. On the other hand, there is also less oxygen, which could impair muscular performance more directly and strongly.

When researchers placed hummingbirds in a chamber in which the oxygen level was reduced and replaced with nitrogen gas, the birds' performance did not suffer significantly. Because the atmospheric density was the same under the two conditions, it follows that the reduced muscular performance at high altitudes may not be the result of the low-oxygen, or hypoxic, conditions per se. Rather, the loss of accelerating capacity and higher wing-stroke amplitudes appear to have more to do with adaptation to low atmospheric density, with its lower aerodynamic lift potential.

Hypoxia may nonetheless become a factor when viewed in conjunction with sugar availability. The amount of plant nectar available to humming-birds does tend to decrease at higher altitudes. At certain times during the year, hypoxia plus low sugar availability may combine to constrain the muscular performance of a high-altitude hummingbird.

Hummingbirds also have very large numbers of mitochondria in their flight muscles. This helps provide a kind of "structural" explanation for the high oxygen requirements for hovering. Scientists can get an idea of the so-called oxidative capacity of a tissue, such as muscle cells or brain cells, by looking at the percentage of the volume of the cell that is taken up by mitochondria, which use oxygen to make chemical energy. Hummingbird flight muscles contain between 28 and 37 percent mitochondria by volume. This is very high.

Hummingbird muscles also receive especially abundant supplies of blood and appear to be able to transfer oxygen very efficiently. They contain very dense structures of tiny blood vessels, known as capillaries. The mitochondria in the muscles are not just more abundant but are located especially near to the blood vessels. This allows the mitochondria to extract oxygen from the blood very rapidly. Hummingbird muscles also contain large amounts of myoglobin, which is like a storage buffer for oxygen. Just as hemoglobin transports oxygen and holds onto it in the blood, myoglobin can store oxygen temporarily in the muscles. Myoglobin also helps transport oxygen from the blood to the muscles.

A host of physical adaptations make hummingbirds virtual flying machines, able to feed efficiently at hard-to-reach food sources. The collared inca gathers nectar from flowers throughout the Andean rain forest.

Metabolism and Muscles

Hummingbird physiology is remarkable both among birds and animals as a whole. For example, hummingbirds are among the tiniest warm-blooded vertebrates. And the metabolic rates of hummingbirds, when viewed on a per-unit-of-body-mass basis, are higher than those of almost any other animal.

Hummingbird hearts also beat very rapidly, providing the birds with a more familiar kind of cardiovascular robustness, but their muscular metabolic machinery is clearly set up to demand and capitalize on their oxygen-delivering capacities.

Similarly, the hearts of hummingbirds, which are very large and beat extremely rapidly, are double the size that researchers would expect on the basis of the birds' body sizes. The heart rate of a hummingbird may reach as high as 1,400 beats per minute—a very high rate—when the hummingbird is flying horizontally or accelerating. When hummingbirds are perching, however, the heart rate may be only 420 beats per minute. During torpor, the heart rates of blue-throated and magnificent hummingbirds are between 36 and 140 beats per minute. Additionally, the amount of oxygen that can be processed by the lungs of hummingbirds is ten times the amount that would be predicted, based on body size.

Hummingbirds also display some larger-scale physical characteristics that help them in flight. For example, the upper arms of hummingbirds' wings are fairly short, but the bones in their hands are long. This is thought to help them attain their high wing-beat frequencies. Some of the bones supporting the tail are also thought to be shaped in a way that helps a hummingbird stay balanced during hovering flight. Additionally, the pectoral or flight muscles, which make up between 25 and 35 percent of the hummingbird's body mass, are exceptionally large and contribute significantly to the flapping motion of the wings. No other bird has flight muscles that make up such a high percentage of its body mass.

Entering Torpor

Although hummingbirds are extremely energetic and proficient in their flight, they also have the capacity to reduce their metabolic rate by entering torpor. Reducing their metabolic rates by as much as 95 percent can help these birds conserve metabolic resources. The body temperatures of hummingbirds, during torpor, can decrease by 68 degrees F. As would be expected, the rate of oxygen consumption, an indication of the metabolic rate, also decreases significantly during torpor.

Hummingbirds tend to exhibit night, or nocturnal, torpor. At night, the air temperature is low, and heating their bodies to a constant temperature would be very costly from a metabolic standpoint. They are also less likely to be preyed upon at night.

Although torpor may appear to lower the metabolic rates of hummingbirds to perilously low levels, the body temperatures of hummingbirds are also able to rapidly rise again. For example, scientists found that the physiological cues of rufous hummingbirds often allow them go into torpor relatively late in their sleep cycles. This allows their usual wake-up time, in the morning, to bring them out of torpor and thereby limit the duration of torpor.

Hummingbirds appear to use torpor more at different times of the year and more when their bodies require more stored energy. When food is less abundant, hummingbirds are more likely to enter torpor. For example, rufous hummingbirds, weighing more in the fall, enter torpor more frequently. In the spring, when the birds weigh less, they do not enter torpor as often. Although weight loss might appear to indicate that a bird is short on fuel and in need of torpor to conserve energy, this is not really the way it works. The body essentially allows itself to waste energy and lose weight when energy sources are abundant. On the flip side, the energy shortages posed by winter will tend to put the metabolism on alert, resulting in more frequent use of torpor to conserve energy and put on weight.

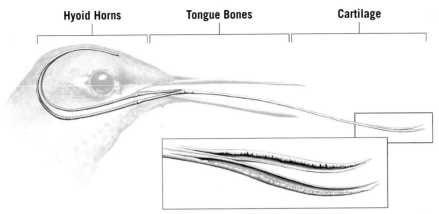

A hummingbird's tongue can move rapidly because of a large, coiled muscle in the skull. The tongue's surface is covered with tiny grooves that carry nectar to the bird's esophagus.

NECTAR CONSUMPTION

Nectar consumption by hummingbirds accomplishes more than providing them with sustenance. Hummingbirds are the largest plant-pollinating organisms in the animal kingdom.

The tongues of hummingbirds are forked at the tips and display grooves along the length of the tongue that allow nectar to be drawn from a flowering plant. A cross section of the hummingbird tongue shows that the structure is very complex and loops around on itself to create grooves. The tongue is not simply a flat surface with small indentations. The grooves on the tongue are narrow enough to allow fluid to move along the tongue by a capillary mechanism. This type of motion is a spontaneous process and results from a force of attraction, or adhesion, of the water in the nectar with the sides of the grooves on the tongue. The nectar nonetheless has to be swallowed after it is spontaneously drawn up the grooves, so there is some energy that must be expended in the overall trip from flower to stomach.

Feeding

Hummingbirds, which make between thirteen and seventeen licks per second during feeding, use their bills to remove the nectar from their tongues. Essentially, the grooves on the tongue are "filled" with each lick. The bill then becomes constricted after each lick in a way that removes, or unloads, nectar from the tongue, and transports it into the esophagus, allowing the birds to swallow it. The removal of the nectar prepares the tongue for another lick, or "licking cycle." The grooves transport most of the nectar that hummingbirds consume (less than 10 percent of the nectar that is obtained at any given time is deposited in droplets on the surface of the tongue and not in the grooves). A hummingbird can also extend its tongue far out past the end of its bill, but most hummingbirds do not usually need to do this.

The hummingbird, like many other birds, has a crop, which is a part of the esophagus that can bulge out and store fluid or other food. The crops of nestling hummingbirds often stick out very dramatically. Scientists generally regard the crops of hummingbirds as being very large in comparison with the crops of other birds. The volume of a hummingbird's crop is between three and ten times the volume of a typical meal. Many hummingbirds do, however, often eat meals that are large enough to temporarily fill up their crops. Usually, however, they tend to fill their crops about halfway full during one feeding event.

The fairly straight bill shapes of temperate hummingbirds generally allow them to feed on numerous types of flowers. North American hummingbirds do feed on the same types of flowers from year to year, but these hummingbirds do not have rigid and exclusive species-specific pollinating relationships with one plant or another. North American hummingbirds feed from a large variety of plants. Researchers cataloged about 127 species of

The downward curve of the green hermit's bill allows the bird to more easily take nectar from long, curved flowers.

Concentrations of Sugar in Nectar and Hummingbird Pollination

Researchers have found that hummingbirds generally consume nectar from flowers with relatively low nectar concentrations, but the reason for this is not entirely clear. The plants that hummingbirds visit generally produce nectar in which the concentration of sugars is between 20 and 25 percent. One explanation for this is that as the sugar concentration increases, the nectar becomes more viscous and cannot be licked as rapidly as nectar with a lower concentration. This is because thicker, more viscous nectar travels up the grooves on the birds' tongues more slowly. But this does not explain the fact that hummingbirds in laboratories generally choose nectar with much higher concentrations, sometimes as high as 65 percent sugars by mass.

Scientists have sometimes assumed that hummingbirds choose more dilute nectar in the wild because it can be consumed more rapidly and can thereby help limit the energy expended in hovering while the birds are licking. More recently, however, the evidence has suggested that hummingbirds are simply not that picky about finding high sugar concentrations, in part because they must expend energy in looking for plants with more concentrated nectar. Hummingbirds also generally tend to consume relatively small volumes of nectar at any given time. By feeding in brief bouts and by not being too choosy about nectar—unless it's provided in high concentrations in the laboratory—hummingbirds may thus be able to minimize their exertion in flight and still obtain adequate amounts of nectar.

flowering plants in the western United States that depend heavily or exclusively on hummingbirds for pollination. Many or most of these plants are perennial plants, meaning that one plant blooms and produces flowers for multiple years and does not need to be replanted or reseeded.

In contrast, some tropical hummingbirds do have bills that allow them to feed especially easily on specific types of flowers. For example, the sword-billed hummingbird, a large hummingbird that lives in Ecuador, has a large bill that lets the bird obtain nectar from a tube-shaped flower that is too long for any other species of hummingbird to extract nectar from. Similarly, the pronounced downward curve of the bill of the white-tipped sicklebill hummingbird, a species that lives in Panama and Costa Rica, allows the bird to obtain nectar from flowers that are also curved. The bill of this hummingbird is extremely curved into almost a half-circular shape.

Brief Feeding Intervals

Hummingbirds only spend about 20 to 25 percent of their time flying around to feed on nectar. In contrast, the birds spend about 75 percent of their time sitting on branches or other perches. Hummingbirds do feed frequently, but each feeding interval may be very short and only provide them with a tiny amount of nectar. Rufous hummingbirds, for example, tend to feed between fourteen and eighteen times per hour, with each feeding interval providing them with about 70 microliters of nectar (about 1.4 percent of a teaspoon). Over the course of an hour, however, the total nectar intake can average out to about 1 milliliter, a more respectable 20 percent of a teaspoon.

It is important to note, however, that a hummingbird will sometimes eat a large amount of nectar in one feeding. Even hummingbirds that have territories will often binge at the end of the day. According to researchers, hummingbirds that do not have territories often eat very large amounts of nectar at the times they are able to invade another hummingbird's territory.

Scientists estimate that an average hummingbird, with a mass of about 0.14 ounce, may consume between 3.8 and 5 teaspoons of nectar each day. For example, assuming the nectar consumed on a day is between 20 and 25 percent sucrose, scientists estimate that a hummingbird may consume an amount of sugar equal to its own body weight on a given day. This amount of nectar also provides hummingbirds with a very large mass of water.

This large intake of sugar also translates into a very large daily intake of calories in relation to the body weight of a hummingbird. For example, a hummingbird might only take in between 7 and 10 calories per day, but this intake is drastically larger than would be expected on the basis of a hummingbird's body weight. If one were to apply the 10-calorie intake of a hummingbird weighing 0.14 ounce to a human, the human (weighing 154 pounds) would have to eat about 175,000 calories in a day—almost eighty-eight times his or her usual caloric intake.

Hummingbirds also appear to feed for relatively brief intervals because their intestines absorb glucose relatively slowly and in a highly regulated way. Scientists think that hummingbirds may feed for such brief periods to allow time for the absorption of sugars from their intestines. The intestines of hummingbirds allow less passive transport of glucose than the intestines of essentially any other vertebrate. Almost all of the glucose is absorbed by active, energy-requiring transport, and hummingbird intestines have extremely large numbers of these transporters.

Although one might expect hummingbird intestines to allow glucose to be dumped into the bloodstream in an unregulated manner to supply muscles with fuel, the more regulated sugar absorption is necessary for certain reasons. Nectar provides hummingbirds with sugar at a higher concentration than in the blood, but the concentration of sugar in the intestines, after the birds swallow the nectar, is actually lower than the glucose level in the blood. If the birds' intestines allowed passive transport, glucose would

Hummingbirds are often seen in flight, but they spend a greater percentage of their time perched. The oasis hummingbird is native to western Peru.

tend to be spontaneously drawn out of the blood and into the fluid in the intestinal tract. The regulated intestines of hummingbirds thus prevent intestinal "glucose wasting."

Large Fluid Intake
Hummingbirds also appear to take in extraordinary amounts of fluid from nectar. Hummingbirds may consume 3 to 5 times their body weights, over a twelve-hour period, in relatively dilute nectar. Although this large volume of fluid intake occurs regularly in some hummingbirds, researchers found that the Anna's hummingbird tended to eat about 1.6 times its body weight in nectar per day. Nonetheless, 1.6 times the body weight in fluid is about 5 times the amount that researchers had predicted on the basis of the bird's body weight.

The bodies of hummingbirds are also highly adapted to deal with the large amounts of water found in nectar. Remarkably, researchers found that about 78 percent of the water consumed by broad-tailed hummingbirds, in Wyoming, was absorbed from the intestines of the birds. Researchers also think that hummingbirds normally excrete large amounts of urine that is dilute, meaning it is relatively free of sodium, potassium, and other electrolytes. A hummingbird will often excrete an amount of urine per day that is about 80 percent of its body weight.

Although hummingbirds excrete large amounts of water while they are eating nectar, which is during the day, their kidneys are able to conserve water at night. Researchers have noted that hummingbirds could potentially become dehydrated during times of the day in which the birds are not consuming nectar with its high water content. Remarkably, the filtration rates of broad-tailed hummingbirds were found to decrease to zero at night and to gradually increase in the morning. As the birds fed more in the middle of the day, their filtration rates more than tripled from the levels they had demonstrated in the early morning.

Interestingly, these hummingbirds were able to more or less shut down their renal water excretion without demonstrating a significant reduction in body temperature. The major decrease in water excretion and kidney function was thus not part of torpor. Researchers think that the blood vessels supplying the kidneys of hummingbirds, and other birds, are unique and allow the filtration rate to be decreased without starving the cells in the kidneys of blood. In humans, an arrest of kidney function can occur because the blood vessels supplying the kidneys become constricted due to inflammation or some other cause. As the cells become starved for blood and therefore for oxygen, the kidneys lose the ability to function and fail. In hummingbirds, there are mechanisms that decrease the filtration rate but still supply the kidney cells with adequate blood.

Hummingbirds also tend to have very high blood-glucose levels. Researchers have found that the blood-glucose levels in three species of hummingbirds are the highest levels that have been found in any mammal. The fasting blood-glucose levels in Anna's, Costa's, and ruby-throated hummingbirds are about 17 millimoles per liter, which is high in comparison with other birds and nearly three times the fasting glucose levels of humans. After the birds have fed, their blood-glucose levels are even higher, at 42 millimoles per liter. Remarkably, the birds do not show evidence of a concomitant increase in the kind of harmful diabetic change that might be expected in animals with such high blood-glucose levels.

Bill Lengths

The lengths of hummingbird bills vary considerably, and birds with different bill lengths may to some extent pollinate flowers in different ways. Researchers have found that ruby-throated hummingbirds with longer bills are almost always able to obtain nectar from deeper within the flower and to obtain the nectar more rapidly from flowers with relatively wide openings than are birds with shorter bills. Although this is generally true, hummingbirds with smaller bills appear to be able to more rapidly extract nectar from narrow flowers than hummingbirds with longer bills. The narrow opening of the flower makes the larger, longer bills more ponderous to insert, and the larger birds can make so-called "insertion errors." For example, the larger bird may fly in, attempt to insert the bill, and miss the nectar-rich part of the narrow flower, causing the bill to "bounce" off the side of the flower.

Hummingbirds with shorter bills also are likely to have preferential "access" to flowers that are smaller and shorter. Although both small and large hummingbirds can obtain nectar from flowers with short, small tubes formed by the petals, the small flowers provide a very small amount of nectar. Researchers thus think larger hummingbirds will not find it cost-effective from a metabolic or exertional standpoint to obtain tiny amounts of nectar. In contrast, the smaller birds will find it worth the effort. It is likely that this reduces competition for nectar among birds of different species as well as differently sized hummingbirds of the same species living in the same area.

Some tropical hummingbirds have serrated bills, although it is not entirely certain what advantage or function these serrations provide. There is evidence that they may be used to crush rigid outer shells of some small insects, but some scientists think they may be used for so-called "nectar robbing." Hummingbirds do not always obtain nectar by the relatively neat and elegant insertion of their bills, head-on, into the flower. Sometimes hummingbirds will pierce the petals of the flower and rob nectar from deeper stores. This allows the hummingbird to obtain nectar but usually does not allow for pollination to occur. More importantly, nectar robbing may damage a flower in a way that prevents the flower from being a reusable resource of nectar. Even if the capacity for nectar production is retained in a flower from which nectar has been robbed, the flower may not be structurally capable of storing nectar and providing it to other hummingbirds. There is some evidence that hummingbirds with serrated bills are more able to use their serrations for this nectar robbing. Hummingbirds may not only pierce flowers but may sometimes grasp and cut flower petals, and serrated bills may make the cutting of thicker flower structures more possible and efficient. As discussed in chapter 3, however, nectar robbing can sometimes indirectly help plants spread their pollen across larger distances.

IRIDESCENT AND MULTICOLORED FEATHERS

The hummingbird feathers that are most relevant to their flight mechanics are the primary flight feathers, secondary flight feathers, and tail feathers. Hummingbirds have 10 primary flight feathers, 6 secondary flight feathers, and 10 tail feathers. They have a total of about 1,500 feathers, however, on their bodies.

Most hummingbirds are born without feathers but develop their normal coat of feathers at about three weeks after hatching. Young ruby-throated and black-chinned hummingbirds lose their first coat of feathers by the time they are one year old. Most hummingbirds molt annually in the late winter or early spring after the birds have migrated to their winter ranges.

The male violet sabrewing of Central America displays shimmering iridescent plumage typical of many tropical species.

Characteristic Coloration

All male and many female hummingbirds have vivid, iridescent feathers. In males, iridescent feathers are generally thought to have evolved to attract more attention from females during mating. In some South American Andean female hummingbirds, however, scientists found that iridescence was often accompanied by aggression in feeding. In other hummingbird species, the degree of iridescent coloring is also known to be associated with territoriality and dominance. Given that female hummingbirds are not able to establish and defend territories as commonly as males are, the degree of coloring tends to be less in females than in males.

The iridescence of hummingbird feathers is primarily a result of refraction and a phenomenon known as optical interference. The iridescent feathers contain small barbules, which themselves consist of even smaller units, known as platelets. Each platelet actually contains small air pockets that have been embedded in another material. There is evidence that the amounts of air in the platelets and the thicknesses of the platelets are the main factors that dictate the color of an iridescent feather. Barbules can contain between seven and fifteen layers of platelets, and each layer is like a horizontal grid of platelets. Above and below these layers of platelets is another layer that is transparent.

At least part of the dark material surrounding the air pockets consists of melanin. Differences in the melanin contents of barbules are thought to produce subtle variations in iridescent colors. The melanin content of the platelets is thus another variable that helps determine the subtle qualities of the iridescent colors. There is usually a clear distinction, however, between the types of coloration that can be produced by pigments, such as melanin, and the types of colors that are produced by the platelets in iridescent barbules. The iridescent colors are produced mainly by the larger-scale structures in the feathers, not the melanin pigments that are part of the feathers.

When one is looking at the pigmented parts of the feathers, the color of the light that is reflected back is very "pure." When a bird or human looks at the feathers at a slightly different angle, however, such as would be produced when the bird moves, the color shifts to one end of the spectrum. This can make the color seem to sparkle or shift as the bird moves or changes directions.

This coloration, produced by interference, is especially evident when, for example, the head of some hummingbirds is viewed from different angles. For example, the head of a male ruby-topaz hummingbird appears to be an even and bright orange when viewed from above but appears to be nearly black when viewed from the side. The iridescent colors on hummingbirds, particularly on the heads and throats, sometimes do appear to be darkened

The vivid coloration of a male magnificent hummingbird's gorget appears to change when viewed from different angles. The structure of a hummingbird's feathers causes the shift.

or black in photographs from certain angles. This is an extreme example of the way interference produces colors that change in association with changes in the angle from which one views the surface. When there is a smaller change in the viewing angle so that a person views an iridescent color in a way that is slightly more direct, an iridescent color of red will appear to shift to orange. By the same mechanism, the color yellow, when viewed more directly or at a more acute angle, will appear to become more green.

How Interference Works

Interference is a complicated optical phenomenon, but it is possible to get a general idea of the way in which interference produces the exceptionally striking iridescence in hummingbird feathers. Essentially, the air and other material in the platelets influence light the way that two layers of different materials influence light. If you put a piece of transparent tape on a piece of glass, the piece of tape will be more or less transparent, depending on the angle at which you view it. Some of the light reflects off the glass and some reflects off the tape. The actual color is determined by the relative amounts of air and the material, some of which appears to be melanin, surrounding the air. The iridescent colors result from some of the light reflecting off one part,

Leucism—as illustrated in a male Anna's hummingbird—affects a small percentage of hummingbirds as well as other types of birds. Leucistic birds have reduced pigmentation in their feathers.

Iridescence, Territoriality, and Maleness

Iridescence, on the one hand, appears to give some hummingbirds a reproductive advantage by allowing their aggressive flight to be more threatening or making them appear more "male." In Andean hummingbirds, for example, the females that feed less aggressively tend to be either less iridescent or noniridescent, and the aggressively feeding females are iridescent and almost appear to be male.

The reason that aggression and bright coloration often go together in males as well as some females is nonetheless not entirely clear. In two hummingbirds with equal degrees of aggression, brighter coloration may amplify the frightening effect of the aggressive flight and thereby translate into more nectar and more access to females for mating. Some scientists have alternatively suggested that coloration and aggression may somehow be more directly tied to each other on a biological level.

A lack of bright coloration, on the other hand, may make a hummingbird less likely to be chased away by a territorial hummingbird. Although a male often will chase all female hummingbirds, including its mate or mates, from its territory, there is some evidence that males do not as readily chase less brightly colored hummingbirds from their territories. These less brightly colored hummingbirds are typically females but can also include younger males that have not yet developed the same degree of mature brightness that adult males exhibit. A lack of striking, iridescent coloration may thus allow a nonterritorial female or a young male to impinge upon another hummingbird's territory with impunity. It is nonetheless important to note that male hummingbirds in particular, when compared with other birds, generally tend to behave very aggressively toward all birds.

or layer, of the platelet and some reflecting from another part of the platelet. Each platelet is like a double-layered surface.

Another factor is the vane-shaped vanular angle, the V-shaped cross section that is made by the barbules within a barb, one of the V-shaped units making up a feather. Essentially, the barbules do not extend out in a completely flat plane but are sloped, much as the banks of a creek or river are sloped upward toward the opposite banks of the creek or river. If the vanular angle is very steep, the degree of visible iridescence of the feather will be more sensitive to changes in the angle with which one views the feathers. The vanular angles within feathers tend to be different on different parts of a hummingbird's body. This variable does not change the colors of the feathers but influences the way in which the iridescence of the feathers is perceived, by birds or people, at different angles.

BRAIN POWER

Hummingbirds have a remarkable ability to remember the locations and qualities of the nectar of flowers they have previously fed upon. To remember, hummingbirds use the heights of flowers, the locations of flowers in relation to other flowers nearby, and the spatial relationship of some flowers to larger features of the landscape. Since hummingbirds appear to have advanced and highly detailed spatial memories, they appear to make few true errors when scientists test their memories in experiments. Hummingbirds do not only remember the two-dimensional positions of flowers, such as would be seen from an aerial viewpoint. The birds also remember and use the heights of flowers, and researchers have tested their memories by varying the heights of flowers in an experimental setting. Researchers have found that hummingbirds can remember the spatial positions of flowers within a resolution of a few centimeters, meaning flowers an inch or two apart from one another. Hummingbirds routinely feed on several hundred flowers each day.

Remembering Times and Colors

Although hummingbirds appear to depend heavily on the three-dimensional spatial maps of flowers, the birds also use other types of cues to help them feed efficiently. Hummingbirds also remember the times at which they last visited individual flowers. This means that they wait for the nectar stores to be filled again in an individual flower they have previously fed upon. Hummingbirds also use the colors of flowers to remember flowers that are good sources or poor sources of nectar.

Scientists have found that hummingbirds remember good nectar-containing flowers by using spatial relationships more than color relationships, but this doesn't mean the birds have poor memories for colors. The minds of hummingbirds just seem to be set up to rely on spatial cues in particular, so that the birds prefer to use spatial indicators more than the specific shapes or colors of flowers. There is evidence nonetheless that hummingbirds make broad associations with colors and are capable of remembering the colors and shapes of flowers that are good nectar sources. Hummingbirds might associate red with flowers that usually contain ample nectar and yellow or pink with a flower that rarely provides them with nectar.

Hummingbirds use both spatial relationships and color to help them locate food sources. The sparkling violetear forages in territories throughout the Andes.

Scientists have found other evidence that hummingbirds do use colors as cues for feeding behaviors. When scientists were observing rufous hummingbirds competing for nectar in a year when the normal density of flowers was drastically decreased, the hummingbirds tended to try to feed from anything that was red. The hummingbirds aggressively maintained territories around red hummingbird feeders, but the hummingbirds also tried to feed from red objects that were not feeders.

Unique Vision

Certain parts of the hummingbird brain are enlarged, compared with those of other birds, and one of these enlarged areas is thought to help the hummingbird see things clearly while it is hovering. In the hummingbird, the collection of nerve cells at the base of the bird's brain is about three times as large as would be expected on the basis of the bird's body weight. Part of the hummingbird's accessory optic system, this group of nerve cells is involved in the optokinetic reflex, which steadies the visual image of something a moving bird is seeing. Alternatively, the reflex steadies and essentially allows the brain to track some types of moving images when the bird is stationary. In the case of the hummingbird, this enlarged portion of the brain helps it to steady the "image" of a flower that it flies in to feed from. This brain enlargement is especially important for stabilizing an image during slight backward motion. As a result, it helps a hummingbird to clearly see a flower that it is inadvertently moving away from during hovering.

2

Living Environments and Migration

DISTRIBUTION

Hummingbirds, which live in many different types of habitats, respond in flexible ways to variations in the weather. Although different species of temperate hummingbirds do tend to breed in relatively well-defined portions of the continental United States, each species is anatomically set up to feed from many of the same species of flowers that other North American hummingbirds are able to feed on. Many of the plants that are found in hummingbirds' habitats, furthermore, have evolved to allow multiple species of hummingbirds to serve as pollinators. Researchers sometimes explain the similarities among North American temperate hummingbirds in terms of evolutionary convergence. The evolution of plants that North American hummingbirds pollinate can also be regarded as convergent in this context, and the plants and hummingbirds can be said to have undergone coevolution. Although different species of North American hummingbirds tend to have many physiological characteristics in common with one another, each species also tends to prefer certain habitats over others. Despite their similarities, North American hummingbirds, even within a given species, live in remarkably diverse environments.

The Tropics and Subtropics

Most of the 328 species of hummingbirds live in tropical or subtropical latitudes throughout the year, and essentially all hummingbirds winter in subtropical climates. Hummingbirds are known as species of the "New World" because they live only in North America, Central America, and South America and not on other continents. A subtropical latitude is one that is between 30 and 40 degrees north or south of the equator. Certain environments that are present at subtropical latitudes may also be described as subtropical. The Sonoran and Mojave deserts in Southern California, for example, are subtropical deserts. The tropics, or tropical latitudes, are those latitudes that are between 23.5 degrees north and 23.5 degrees south of the

equator. North America technically includes Mexico and therefore includes some tropical latitudes, and a North American hummingbird could conceivably be defined as any one of the multiple species that breeds, at least in some numbers, at any of the subtropical or tropical latitudes within the United States or Mexico. For the sake of discussion in this book, however, the phrase "North American hummingbird" is meant to refer only to the 16 species that routinely breed within the United States.

Decreasing Diversity

Apart from the broader distinction between tropical versus subtropical distributions, the diversity of hummingbirds decreases as the latitude increases north or south of the equator. For example, at 5 degrees north or south of the equator, the tropical environments contain between 158 and 163 species of hummingbirds. Between 55 and 110 species live around 15 degrees north or south of the equator. The diversity of species in South America is slightly stronger at latitudes between 15 and 25 degrees south of the equator than the diversity is at the same distances north of the equator. In the Northern Hemisphere, only about 19 species live at latitudes around 25 degrees north, whereas about 61 species live in the vicinity of 25 degrees south.

Sixteen species of hummingbirds are North American species that breed at various locations in the United States and southern Canada. Many of these species generally winter in Mexico or in locations farther south, such as in Central American countries. Rufous hummingbirds winter in Mexico and, to a lesser extent, in the southeastern United States and breed as far north as southern Alaska. Some ruby-throated hummingbirds also winter in the southeastern United States, generally along the southern coasts of Texas and Florida. Anna's hummingbirds also sometimes winter in western Texas and then breed in California or at sites farther north. Some North American hummingbirds, such as the buff-bellied and ruby-throated hummingbirds, also breed in Florida and across the states along the Gulf coast. The breeding and wintering ranges of the ruby-throated hummingbird can thus overlap, for the species as a whole, in states such as Texas and Florida.

The breeding areas of some North American species are distributed across large areas of North America. The ruby-throated hummingbird has the largest distribution of any North American hummingbird and breeds across all the eastern and midwestern United States and most of the southern portions of the eastern provinces of Canada. Although the ruby-throated hummingbird is the only species whose normal breeding range extends

Tropical hummingbird species include more elaborately plumed birds than do more northern species. The male booted racket-tail of South America sports eye-catching tail-feather tufts and white feathered "boots."

through many midwestern and northeastern states, this does not mean that other species are never present in these states. Several other North American species have been seen breeding or even wintering at points across most of the eastern half of the United States outside their normal ranges. Black-chinned hummingbirds also have a large distribution, and some of them breed as far south as Mexico or as far north as Canada. Three other species that breed in parts of Canada, mostly within the central and western parts of British Columbia, are Anna's, calliope, and rufous hummingbirds. Most Anna's hummingbirds, however, breed in California, Arizona, and on the Baja peninsula of Mexico. Many Anna's hummingbirds also breed in southern California during the winter months and then travel relatively small distances for the summer to locations in the mountains of California or Arizona. Although calliope hummingbirds have something of a preference for mountainous habitats and can breed in parts of Canada, many of them also breed in central and southern California.

Although at least five species of hummingbirds do routinely breed in Canada, most North American species normally breed in the western and southwestern states. Broad-tailed hummingbirds breed in Nevada and the four corners states and also in most portions of Mexico. Allen's, Costa's, broad-billed, and blue-throated hummingbirds mostly breed in the southwestern states of Arizona, New Mexico, Texas, and California. The breeding territories of the buff-bellied hummingbird correspond to most of the coast of the Gulf of Mexico, from the Yucatan peninsula into western Florida, and do not extend very far inland. Other North American hummingbirds only generally breed as far north as southeastern Arizona and southwestern New Mexico. These species include lucifer, magnificent, berylline, white-eared, and violet-crowned hummingbirds.

Nonmigrating Species

Some hummingbirds live in the continental United States throughout the year and do not migrate. For example, Allen's and Anna's hummingbirds are the main breeding species in the San Francisco area. Many members of these hummingbird species live in southern California throughout the year, although more Anna's than Allen's hummingbirds live throughout the year in the United States. Some Anna's hummingbirds also live year-round throughout the coastal sections of Oregon and Washington.

Some Anna's and Allen's hummingbirds and members of two other species, Costa's and black-chinned hummingbirds, also breed and live year-round in the Los Angeles area. Rufous hummingbirds migrate through southern California but do not generally breed there. Many Anna's hummingbirds, however, live year-round in the Los Angeles area and nest for six months out of the year, between mid-December and the middle of June. As noted above, however, some Anna's hummingbirds may finish nesting during the late winter and then travel into other parts of California, such as into the mountains, for the summer. There is evidence that this long, potential breeding season allows some Anna's hummingbirds to nest three—not the more typical two—times a year. Other Anna's hummingbirds live farther north, however, and do not start building their nests until April or later. Hummingbirds generally nest when they are able to relatively consistently obtain nectar and other sources of food, and this may mean nesting later at more northern latitudes.

Some rufous hummingbirds nest at locations that are farther north than the sites at which other North American hummingbirds nest. For example, some rufous hummingbirds breed as far north as Alaska and migrate the full 3,000 or more miles between Alaska and Mexico, twice a year.

Expanding Ranges

More and more rufous hummingbirds have been gradually moving, in increasing numbers, into the eastern United States. Most rufous humming-birds breed in the Pacific Northwest in the summer as far south as Oregon and Idaho and as far north as Alaska. Most of them then migrate south and winter in northwestern Mexico and the central portion of Mexico. Scientists and others are noticing, however, that more and more rufous humming-birds spend their winters along the coast of the Gulf of Mexico, in Texas, Louisiana, Mississippi, and Florida. These hummingbirds also winter in, or pass through in the late fall, states such as Alabama and Tennessee. This east-ward extension of the distribution of rufous hummingbirds is relatively "recent," given that a researcher first reported a rufous hummingbird win-tering east of the Mississippi in 1909. The numbers of them that have been seen wintering in eastern states has increased exponentially since 1990. Before the late 1980s and early 1990s, very few people reported seeing rufous hummingbirds in winter in the southeastern states in any given year.

The development of suburban vegetation in the southeastern states over the last hundred years has, researchers think, interacted with the evolution of hummingbirds' inherited "flight compasses." If even a few birds had inher-ited a compass that made them fly a little bit more southeast than south, it is likely that the newly developed and deforested southeastern states would then have provided them with good wintering grounds. It is unlikely that rufous hummingbirds spontaneously or haphazardly moved into the south-east; hummingbirds migrate with precision and do not generally follow one another around on migration routes. Parts of Mexico may also have become less desirable, partly as a result of deforestation, as wintering grounds for rufous hummingbirds.

Why do hummingbirds migrate? There is no one definitive answer, but scientists think that one reason for migration is that there is more daylight in the spring and summer at more northern latitudes than there is at equatorial latitudes. Another factor that may have favored the evolution of migratory behavior is the sheer density of species and numbers of hummingbirds in the

Researchers have noted a pronounced movement of rufous hummingbirds into the eastern United States. Thirty years ago, very few were seen wintering in the East; winter sightings are much more common today.

tropics. Because there are so many hummingbirds and insects, many of whom would impinge upon a hummingbird's feeding territory if given the chance, it is likely to be advantageous for a hummingbird to nest and reproduce in the less-crowded and more "wide-open" land that is farther north.

Numerous species of hummingbirds live on various Caribbean islands, including the Greater and Lesser Antilles, Trinidad and Tobago, the Bahamas, Puerto Rico, and Hispaniola. Some ruby-throated hummingbirds evidently migrate south along the Florida Keys and through Cuba and may interact with some of these island communities of tropical hummingbirds.

TYPES OF LIVING ENVIRONMENTS

The living environments of North American hummingbirds could be separated into winter, stopover, and breeding environments, but many hummingbirds live in many different types of environments. It is not necessarily appropriate to divide hummingbird habitats into rigidly defined categories, given that many migratory hummingbirds are more or less on the move for much of the year. Although hummingbirds do breed in a specific location, they often only remain in the area for a month or two and will then begin migrating south. And rufous hummingbirds, as an example, do not migrate to one site in Mexico and stay there during the winter months. There tends to be a continual movement—south, then west, then north through Mexico—during the fall and winter months.

Researchers typically refer to a habitat as an environment in which certain types of vegetation predominate, and some North American species do tend to prefer environments that are more or less dry or that have more or less dense vegetation. The Costa's hummingbird tends to live in the true, open desert and is known for living in drier areas than other North American species live in. That said, most species seem to prefer living somewhere near a river or stream. In the desert, for example, Costa's hummingbirds may nest near an intermittent stream, one that carries water some of the time. Most North American species tend to nest in mixed coniferous and deciduous forests, at elevations between 3,000 and 8,000 feet. Blue-throated hummingbirds seem to nest in densely forested areas, but most other species live in parts of forests that have clearings or that are not especially dense with trees.

Altitudinal and Latitudinal Movements

Some species move to lower altitudes in a seasonal fashion, typically in the winter, and these species may or may not be regarded as altitudinal migrants. The calliope hummingbird moves to lower altitudes in the winter and breeds at fairly high altitudes. Anna's hummingbirds are sometimes viewed as altitudinal migrants, although they move along paths that scientists have not thoroughly pinned down. The berylline hummingbird is another altitudinal migrant, although the migration of some beryllines into the United States is clearly based partially on latitude. Most true altitudinal migrants tend to not breed in the United States, however, and instead live throughout the year in Mexico or more equatorial latitudes. The difference between a seasonal and altitudinal migrant species, moreover, may not be clear. A seasonal migrant may tend to live at different altitudes in the winter and summer, but the migration, such as within part of Mexico, may actually be more latitudinally than altitudinally driven.

In the fall and winter months, North American hummingbirds typically migrate to warm locations in tropical and semitropical areas. Some, however, spend the winter along the northern coast of the Gulf of Mexico or in Florida.

The usual wintering areas include different parts of Mexico and Central America. For example, rufous hummingbirds are known to breed in states in the Pacific Northwest and then begin migrating during the late summer months. After they migrate south, they live and feed in various parts of Mexico. When the birds are migrating, they make several stops and set up temporary stopover territories. Rufous hummingbirds begin migrating surprisingly early in the summer and usually arrive in the Sierra Nevada of California, for example, by the end of July and the beginning of August. Rufous hummingbirds typically migrate south along paths that are farther east than California. But a rufous hummingbird migrating south through Arizona will typically arrive at about the same latitude, at about the same time, as a rufous hummingbird migrating south through eastern California. Within Mexico, North American hummingbirds tend to live in mixed forests at moderate to high elevations.

A Preference for Mountains

Although it is evident that North American hummingbirds move through and live in many different ecological habitats, many of these species do tend to prefer mountainous environments in the western portion of North America. Among tropical hummingbirds that live in South America there is a larger variety of species living in the higher altitudes than there is at lower altitudes. Even the desert environments within the Colorado plateau, which spans parts of the four corners states, are at a high elevation. Broad-tailed hummingbirds breed across the relatively high altitudes of the deserts of Arizona, Nevada, and New Mexico, and parts of Arizona are important stopover sites for rufous hummingbirds. The broad-tailed and calliope hummingbirds are two species that generally live and nest at the highest elevations, often above 10,000 feet.

Why do North American hummingbirds tend to move through and breed at higher elevations? It is puzzling because temperatures are cooler, especially at night, at high altitudes. The small body sizes of hummingbirds also give their bodies large surface-area-to-volume ratios, thereby causing them to lose body heat more easily than even a larger bird would lose heat. Hummingbirds clearly migrate along paths that let them take advantage of nectar sources, and this need for nectar sources ends up taking them along paths through high altitudes. But it is not clear why these particular paths, through high altitudes, became established in the evolutionary pasts of both hummingbirds and the flowers that are pollinated by them.

The need for tree sap from holes that have previously been drilled by sapsuckers may help explain the tendency of hummingbirds to nest in specific types of forests. The ruby-throated hummingbird, for example, tends to rely especially heavily on nonnectar sources of food, such as tree sap and insects. The reliance of ruby-throated hummingbirds on tree sap probably explains the birds' preference for forest environments in parts of the country.

Some hummingbirds prefer mountainous regions, even in the United States. The broad-tailed hummingbird breeds in the highest areas—the high-altitude deserts of Arizona, Nevada, and New Mexico.

Researchers think that rufous and ruby-throated hummingbirds, particularly in the spring, essentially move along paths and live in types of forests that allow them to eat tree sap from holes drilled by the yellow-bellied sapsucker. Ruby-throated hummingbirds, as well, appear to rely somewhat heavily on jewelweed plants, which are species of plants in the genus *Impatiens*, as a source of nectar to prepare for their southward migrations in the fall. The distribution and habitat preferences of some species of hummingbirds can thus be influenced by the distributions of certain plants, trees, or even other birds.

Life in the Wintering Ranges

During the winter months, many North American hummingbirds compete with members of tropical hummingbird species for access to nectar. Although there is not a great deal of information on the interactions of tropical and North American hummingbird species during the nonbreeding season, there is evidence that North American hummingbirds are often not the dominant species in their wintering environments. Researchers, for example, found that calliope hummingbirds living in Mexico in the winter were not very successful in establishing territories, especially large territories, for feeding. Similarly, rufous hummingbirds breeding in the United States are very dominant over other species, but the same hummingbirds are not usually able to set up territories during the winter in Mexico. Since a large variety of nectar-producing flowers do bloom in the winter in Mexico, nectar tends to be ample.

Many of the tropical species that spend the entire year in parts of Mexico nest and reproduce in Mexico during the summer months. Some of the tropical species do seem to have thus become adapted to breed at times when there is less competition for nectar from migratory hummingbirds, given that many migratory hummingbirds are not present in southern Mexico in the summer. This is noteworthy, in part, because the absolute amounts of nectar, produced by plants, can actually be lower, in parts of Mexico, in the summer than in the winter.

Competition in Mexico

North American hummingbirds that are wintering in parts of Mexico may have to contend with relatively few other hummingbird species but still have to deal with nectar robbers. The diversity of tropical hummingbird species living in parts of Mexico, particularly during the winter months, can be surprisingly low. In western Mexico, near Guadalajara, researchers found that wintering black-chinned, rufous, broad-tailed, violet-crowned, and calliope hummingbirds fed in the same area during many of the winter months, between November and March. During these months, only four other resident species of hummingbirds (species that lived in the area year-round) and three other migrant tropical species of hummingbirds (species that had migrated from sites within Mexico or Central America) were present.

Both the wintering North American and resident or migrant tropical hummingbirds had to deal with nectar robbing from at least two other species of birds that were not hummingbirds. These nectar-robbing birds visited most of the same plants that the hummingbirds fed from and pollinated. Members of these nectar-robbing species of birds also sometimes served, unwittingly, as pollinators of the plants they robbed nectar from. Even though North American hummingbirds wintering in Mexico may not have to compete with dozens of tropical hummingbird species, the feeding environments can nonetheless be complex. Hummingbirds always outnumbered the nectar robbers—sometimes by more than sixtyfold, usually by about tenfold—but the nectar robbers were still very active.

STOPOVER ENVIRONMENTS AND TERRITORIES

During migration, each stop typically lasts between one and three weeks and allows the hummingbirds to regain weight lost during flights. Although some stopovers may be as brief as four days, hummingbirds tend to be very thin and weakened after a long flight and often need more time to regain weight. A hummingbird can easily lose 0.071 ounce of body fat on a single, nonstop migratory flight—a significant portion of the hummingbird's body weight. Setting up a stopover territory is not really a casual experience for a hummingbird, given that hummingbirds will often compete fiercely for access to flowers in, for example, a mountain clearing. A hummingbird that cannot establish its own stopover territory will be forced to impinge upon another hummingbird's territory.

The Importance of Flowers

Scientists have found that the quality of flowers, in terms of nectar provision and the number of flowers, varies greatly from year to year along a given migratory route. This can make the task of setting up a stopover territory all the more complex. Rufous hummingbirds, for example, had lower average body weights, when the scientists captured them briefly in nets and weighed them, in the years when the quality of flowers was low. In years of low rainfall, the favorite flowers of hummingbirds lacked in nectar production because they dried out.

The health of rufous and other North American hummingbirds may depend on weather and rainfall patterns across a large area of the Rocky Mountains, Cascades, and Sierra Nevada. Abundant winter snowfall in the Sierra Nevada may help insulate some plants from excessive cold, thereby allowing the plants to flower more robustly in the spring and summer months. Normal amounts of winter snow also provide meltwater in the spring. Researchers found that when the snowfall was poor in the winter, there was a delay in the time at which the flowers bloomed most abundantly. The qualities of stopover habitats are therefore quite sensitive to changes in the amounts and timing of precipitation and to the time and rate at which the weather warms in the spring.

Differences in rainfall, even across different parts of an apparently homogeneous environment, may affect the sites at which hummingbirds establish stopover territories or live on a more permanent basis. The Sonoran Desert of Arizona, for example, can contain a greater diversity of hummingbird species than the drier Mojave Desert in southern California.

The sizes of stopover territories can vary much more than the total quantity of flowers within each territory. Researchers, for example, analyzed the stopover territories of rufous hummingbirds in Arizona when the hummingbirds were stopping on their southward migrations in late July and found that some territories were a hundred times larger than others. Across these territories, however, the flower number per territory ranged from 301 to 1,699. This is a much smaller degree of variation. Hummingbirds apparently have a remarkable ability to vary the geographical sizes of their territories to meet their daily nectar requirements.

Conservation Issues

Many tropical hummingbird species appear to be able to respond fairly well to the breaking up of the rain forest with cattle ranges and logging and the like, but other indications suggest that people should be concerned about the fragmentation of the rain forest. As the continuous rain forest has become fragmented, or interrupted by farmland and grazing land, the populations of many species of birds have been shown to be reduced in the vicinity of the fragmented forests. In the Amazonian rain forest in Brazil, however, researchers found that the sizes of the populations of nine species of hummingbirds did not decrease in response to fragmentation of the forest. One reason that many hummingbirds may be able to adapt to these changes is that the tropical hummingbirds are known to fly large distances from flower to flower, meaning that they can and do expand their foraging habitats across gaps in the forest. For example, tropical species of hummingbirds of the genus *Phaethornis*, which are hermit hummingbirds, have been shown to routinely fly between a quarter and a half a mile from one flower to the next one. Nonetheless, the Brace's emerald hummingbird is one species that has become extinct in the last century, and scientists view twenty species as being either critically endangered or endangered. Scientists regard eight more species as being "vulnerable" to extinction. Given that hummingbirds are not hunted by humans or exposed to another major source of direct and unnatural mortality, it is reasonable to assume that ecological disruptions have decreased the populations of these species.

Some human actions can enhance the survival of different hummingbird populations, but others can hurt. Maintaining hummingbird feeders can help prepare the birds for migration or allow weak hummingbirds, ones that have already chosen not to migrate, to survive the winter. Hummingbirds, however, can be exposed to pesticides from lawns or agricultural activities; they also can collide with windows and die.

In some cases, humans produce changes in the landscape that benefit some species of hummingbirds. Some scientists have noted that the creation of unnatural clearings in forests can increase the amount of sunlight reaching the ground and thereby improve the spread and growth of nectar-producing plants. In addition, the growth of some of these same bushes or plants can

The Brazilian ruby thrives along forest edges and in gardens in eastern Brazil.

provide more nesting sites for those species that nest in or near to the ground. Anna's hummingbirds have thus been able to live in larger numbers in the parts of Arizona's Sonoran Desert that have been made locally less like a desert through the planting of trees and grass. Scientists think this same development, however, has probably caused the year-round range of the Costa's hummingbird, a species that lives in the more open desert, to shift and contract.

Even though many species are adaptable to environmental disturbances, changes in the diversities of forest habitats may affect the distributions of some hummingbirds in some areas. Most of the twenty-five species of hummingbirds that were either endangered or vulnerable as of 1999, for example, were known to require a forest environment for their breeding to take place normally. Some species, thus, do have more of a strong preference than others for nesting in dense forests.

Finally, several North American species are wintering more along the Gulf coast of the United States, which may be due to the actions of humans in either Mexico or the Southeast. It is possible that changes in Mexican forests have caused these species to be less able to winter in Mexico; however, the increases in the numbers of feeders or in the growth of nectar-producing plants, in gardens or in the less-dense forests of the suburbs, may simply be providing these species with better areas for winter feeding.

THE CHALLENGE OF MIGRATION

Hummingbirds migrate alone and follow routes that are very long and often quite dangerous. Young hummingbirds moreover do not receive any real guidance in migration from their mothers. As a group, the young birds often begin migrating later than adult hummingbirds do. Although the overall directionality of migration is driven by responses to biological cues—such as changes in the light or in weather—and not by social cues, members of a given species do tend to follow remarkably similar migratory paths. It is important to note, however, that hummingbirds do not migrate in groups.

Weather's Impact

A hummingbird may also alter the timing of a migratory step in response to changes in weather or the availability of food. Hummingbirds appear to be able to effectively use the weather to their advantage. Differences in the weather, either between migratory seasons or within a given year, may nonetheless impair the availability of nectar or insects at various points along a migration route. Researchers have noted that a spring snowstorm, as an example, can severely reduce, albeit temporarily, both nectar production and the availability of insects for food.

Hummingbirds also adjust their migrations in response to seasonal and more short-term weather changes. Researchers, for example, saw larger numbers of ruby-throated hummingbirds migrating south, through the Appalachian Mountains, on days when the wind was blowing from the north to the south. Ruby-throated hummingbirds also traveled more when the wind speeds, blowing from north to south, were higher. Using tailwinds to improve their flight efficiencies is probably therefore a factor in helping ruby-throated hummingbirds to migrate more rapidly than members of other hummingbird species. Even though ruby-throated hummingbirds do not make very long stopovers, they are able to adjust their migrations to capitalize on short-term changes in the weather. Ruby-throated hummingbirds also tend to make migratory flights in the middle of the day, but this approach probably has more to do with feeding strategies than with weather. If the hummingbirds began flying early in the morning, their blood sugar levels would be too low to allow them to fly efficiently. If they flew into the evening hours, they would potentially be unable to feed in preparation for sleep.

The age and sex of a hummingbird often impact the timing of migration. Adult male hummingbirds essentially always begin their fall migration earlier, typically about two to six weeks earlier, than do adult females. Young hummingbirds typically begin migrating later than the adult females. Researchers noted in one study that juvenile male Allen's hummingbirds in California were the last to migrate and began migrating two weeks after all

Wing-Disc Loading and
Long-Distance Flight

Researchers have generally found that territorial hummingbirds have bodies that are built more for brief, aggressive flight displays than for the most efficient hovering or long-distance flight. This is especially striking in rufous hummingbirds. The wing-disc loading—the bird's mass divided by the wing area—of rufous hummingbirds is the greatest of any temperate hummingbird species, but rufous hummingbirds migrate longer distances than any other temperate species. Surprisingly, hummingbirds with greater wing-disc loading fly less efficiently and require more energy to hover or fly long distances. Perhaps rufous hummingbirds are able to fly and maneuver across short distances, such as in chasing intruders from their territories, more efficiently with their relatively shorter wings. Either shorter wings or a larger body mass will tend to increase wing-disc loading. Put simply: aggressive and efficient chasing is more evolutionarily advantageous for territorial hummingbirds than very efficient migratory or hovering flight. An extension of this interpretation, however, is that rufous hummingbirds can be more likely to survive migration by being very aggressive in establishing stopover territories. This aggressive refueling can therefore make up for less-efficient migratory flight.

Researchers have recently noted that wing-disc loading should probably not be used as the only variable in analyzing the relationships between foraging approaches and flight efficiencies. Different hummingbirds are nonetheless able to use their physical characteristics to gain advantages in feeding.

of the adult females had gone. In the spring or breeding season, male hummingbirds also tend to arrive in their breeding environments before females.

Remarkable Distances

Rufous hummingbirds have the longest migrations, on average, of any species of hummingbird and have to deal with many harsh environments. Rufous hummingbirds have to migrate long distances across deserts and other portions of land that do not have any sources of nectar. Despite these challenges, many hummingbirds migrate successfully and, perhaps more notably, often follow a route that is very similar from year to year.

The ruby-throated hummingbird is remarkable in its ability to cross the Gulf of Mexico in a single flight. It must fly, at a minimum, between 457 and

528 miles without stopping. Flights of ruby-throated hummingbirds across the Gulf of Mexico are sometimes as long as 621 miles. Ruby-throated hummingbirds sometimes perch on oil platforms as far as 205 miles from the coast, but it is unlikely that resting on an oil platform really shortens a hummingbird's flight. Even if a hummingbird were able to stop at the same platform year after year, there would be no reliable source of food on the platform. Ruby-throated hummingbirds may more commonly fly north, rather than south, across the Gulf of Mexico. This has been explained by the fact that the hummingbirds could potentially miss the target of the Yucatán peninsula and hit land either southwest or southeast of the peninsula, thereby making their flights longer.

Although some observers have reported seeing ruby-throated hummingbirds flying very low over the water of the Gulf of Mexico, there is evidence that these hummingbirds may initially fly fairly high up when they are still over land and then set out over the water. Some researchers have hypothesized that ruby-throated hummingbirds begin their migrations across the Gulf of Mexico a significant distance inland from the coast.

Hummingbirds can migrate at a maximum speed of between about 25 and 27 mph, and scientists have found that hummingbirds can fly fairly rapidly for long distances. A banded rufous hummingbird in Montana, for example, flew 747 miles to Colorado in between six and nine days. When

The ruby-throated hummingbird, North America's most widespread species, makes a spectacular migration—flying across the Gulf of Mexico, a distance of some 500 miles, without stopping.

researchers factored in the time that the bird had spent stopping to eat and replenish its energy reserves, it was clear that the hummingbird had flown the entire 747-mile distance in between one and three days. Researchers noted that the hummingbird had been able to fly at least about 373 miles at a stretch. The "range" of a hummingbird is defined as the distance the bird can fly in one flight. The real-world range of the ruby-throated hummingbird, for example, is about 606 to 621 miles. The theoretical range of a ruby-throated hummingbird, in the absence of any wind, has been estimated to be as high as 1,491 miles. This estimate is based on the fact that ruby-throated hummingbirds become very obese before migrating and have 40 to 45 percent body fat, calculated in the usual manner as a percent of the wet weight of the body. In other cases, some Allen's and ruby-throated hummingbirds have flown between 472 and 504 miles over periods of thirty-two days. It is important to remember that, during these thirty-two-day periods, these hummingbirds were stopping to eat and regain weight for long stretches of time.

Although some species do not begin their fall migrations until August or September, rufous hummingbirds may begin migrating south as early as July. Many rufous hummingbirds that breed in Idaho and Montana, for example, reach these locations by May and begin to leave in July. Researchers found that these rufous hummingbirds tended to reach northern Mexico by August and southern Mexico by September. They remained in extreme southern Mexico throughout January. In the early spring, many rufous hummingbirds reach northern Mexico by late February and early March and northern California by late April.

Hummingbirds gain large amounts of fat in preparation for migration. Some ruby-throated hummingbirds, which usually weigh about 0.11 ounce, gain up to 0.07 ounce of body fat before they migrate. Hummingbirds may lose much of this extra weight by making a long flight. To regain this lost weight, hummingbirds usually interrupt their migrations for four to seven days at a time, or longer, to eat.

The Return Flight

Many hummingbirds do not follow the same path north in the spring as they do on their southward migrations in the fall. They are often able to migrate along different paths at different elevations, in the spring and fall, and thereby feed on flowers that bloom at different times. Hummingbirds that are migrating north in the spring, for example, often follow routes through relatively low elevations. These routes often extend through parts of the Colorado plateau and the mountain valleys of California. In the fall, the same birds often migrate along routes at higher altitudes in the mountains, given that the flowers that hummingbirds feed from are not in bloom at that time at lower elevations. Rufous hummingbirds, for example, migrate along paths that fit this general pattern. They migrate north through California in the spring and then south, in the late summer and early fall, through the higher elevations of

Studies indicate that calliope hummingbirds make their springtime migration along the Pacific Coast even though that route takes them away from food sources located inland. Avoiding sudden spring storms might be the reason.

Utah, eastern Arizona, and western New Mexico. A typical pattern for a rufous hummingbird is to fly north along the Pacific coast, fly east, in May, and nest in Idaho or western Montana, and then fly south through Colorado and New Mexico. Others, however, continue flying north, enter Canada around May, and breed in Canada or Alaska.

In one study, researchers found that almost all rufous and calliope hummingbirds somewhat inexplicably migrated along the Pacific Coast in the springtime. The strictly defined quality of the springtime coastal path, which can generally be described as the Pacific flyway, is surprising in part because there are nectar-producing plants that flower in the spring along the more inland path that rufous hummingbirds migrate along in the fall. This fall path generally corresponds to the central flyway and includes parts of New Mexico and other inland sites. Researchers think that the hummingbirds may have learned to avoid inclement weather that can produce springtime snowfalls in parts of Arizona and New Mexico, particularly in the mountain environments. Alternatively, researchers have suggested that the coastal springtime path may have become established during the last glacial maximum, the last "ice age," which ended about 12,500 years ago. The hummingbirds may have only recently begun nesting, and migrating south, at more inland sites.

3

Behavior

OBTAINING INSECTS AND TREE SAP

Hummingbirds may be solitary birds and spend the majority of their time perching, but many of them do have to very frequently interact with other birds. Tropical hummingbirds with small territories may have to chase large numbers of intruding hummingbirds away from their plants. Even though the densities of hummingbird populations are lower in many parts of the United States than in Mexico and Central America, hummingbirds have to dynamically maintain mental maps of their nectar sources and very frequently respond to intruders or competitors.

Hummingbirds often have to rely on insects as a substitute for nectar; some species can eat almost exclusively insects at particular times of the year. Hummingbirds, skilled at catching flies and other insects either from leaves or in midair, obtain significant amounts of nourishment from them. Hummingbirds are sometimes not able to consume nectar for relatively long intervals of time, and eating insects can be a viable substitute for nectar as an energy source.

Hummingbirds generally eat insects every day, but different species may either eat more insects or prefer different types of insects. For example, different hummingbirds eat gnats, flies, wasps, bees, ants, and spiders. Researchers have noted that species with more highly curved bills, such as the tropical hermit hummingbirds, tend to eat more flies than birds with less curved bills. Magnificent hummingbirds that breed in the United States often have to eat more insects than nectar.

Catching Insects

Different species of hummingbirds use different flight strategies to obtain insects for food. Long-tailed hermit and little hermit hummingbirds in Costa Rica, for example, use hover-gleaning to obtain insects. Hover-gleaners obtain most of their insects by flying up to a spiderweb and plucking the spiders or other insects out of the web. These species typically visit webs that are between 1.7 and 17 feet above the ground in tropical forests. Many North American species use more than one approach to eat insects. Broad-billed hummingbirds are known to use both gleaning and hawking, for example, and buff-bellied hummingbirds glean and use other means to catch insects.

Other flight strategies for obtaining insects are sally-gleaning, sally-hawking, and hover-hawking. Scientists sometimes refer to these terms loosely as sallying and hawking, but the three specific behaviors can still be regarded as distinct from one another. In sally-gleaning, a hummingbird perched on a branch will fly upward, pluck an insect off a leaf, and return to its branch. In sally-hawking, a hummingbird perched on a branch will fly up from the branch, catch an insect flying by the branch, and then return to the perching site. In hover-hawking, a hummingbird, flying around in a zigzag pattern, catches insects that are in flight.

These various behaviors can be understood in terms of the individual words that describe the behaviors. Hawking refers to the catching of insects that are flying, and gleaning refers to the capturing of insects that are moving on a spiderweb or a leaf or other surface. A hummingbird can be hovering while doing this or sallying, meaning that the bird is perched at the beginning and end of the gleaning or hawking. A sally is defined as a sudden movement outward, such as when a military unit goes out from its camp on a sortie and then returns. Hummingbirds that are perching thus may appear to be at rest but are still likely to be alert to passing food.

Hummingbirds, although good at catching insects, often appear less than elegant in their insect-catching behaviors. In forests, hummingbirds sometimes glean insects from very dense foliage that is low to the ground. They are also able to glean insects from either side of a leaf, and this may require somewhat precise feats of flight. Researchers think that as hummingbirds are gleaning, they will sometimes force insects out into the open with the movements of their wings. Once the insects are out, a hummingbird may then eat the insect, in the open, by sally-hawking or hover-hawking. If an insect is large, a hummingbird may also not immediately swallow or completely catch the insect. Researchers, for example, have sometimes observed hummingbirds sallying to catch insects, flicking the insects out of their mouths haphazardly, and then flying up to catch the potentially incapacitated insects again.

The saliva and tongues of hummingbirds may also help them catch insects. The very thick saliva may essentially be sticky enough to act like a crude form of flypaper. The tips of hummingbird tongues, as noted previously, are forked, and a hummingbird can move the forked portion somewhat independently of the rest of its tongue. The birds may add some precision to their insect-catching techniques with these tongue movements.

Hummingbirds appear to develop habits for obtaining insects that allow them to minimize energy expenditure and maintain the integrities of their territories. Male hummingbirds, for example, appear to rely on sallying

The snowcap, like most hummingbirds, might be searching for food even when it's perched. Hummingbirds often make quick flights to nab an insect from a leaf or out of midair before returning to a perch.

when they are perched on branches and monitoring their territories. A male hummingbird might perch near to the flowers within its territory that are most nectar rich. When insects pass by, the hummingbird, expending only a small amount of energy, can keep an eye on its flowers as it sallies to catch an insect.

Hummingbirds also migrate at times that will perhaps allow them to have access to enough insects for food. It makes sense that the blooming of flowers, when the weather becomes warm in the spring, would be accompanied by increases in the population densities of, and movements of, insects.

Hummingbirds also consume sap from trees, usually by using holes that sapsuckers have already drilled. Researchers have observed five of the species of North American hummingbirds flying around with sapsuckers, which are types of woodpeckers, and then eating sap out of the sapsuckers' holes. There is evidence that rufous and ruby-throated hummingbirds depend heavily on sap from trees, particularly when the hummingbirds first reach their springtime breeding areas in different parts of North America.

Sex Differences in Territorial Defense

Although female hummingbirds wield significant "power" in choosing males to mate with, male hummingbirds are more able to maintain desirable feeding territories than are females. Among rufous hummingbirds in California, researchers noted that young, male hummingbirds were generally dominant, in terms of feeding, over both young females and adult females. When the availabilities of nectar-rich flowers decreased in the territories of male hummingbirds, for example, the males tended to more aggressively enlarge their territories into neighboring areas. Males also tended to have territories that were more densely packed with flowers than were the territories of females. Finally, immature females were never successful at keeping adult females away and were generally unsuccessful at chasing away males of any age.

Rufous hummingbirds maintain a fairly clear hierarchy of dominance, based on age and sex, and the reasons for this are surprisingly unclear. Young males often pushed young females out of parts of the females' territories and, less commonly, pushed some other young males out. When young males were pushed from their territories, the displacements were, however, most commonly accomplished by adult males and were not accomplished by females of any ages. Rufous hummingbirds of both sexes and all ages aggressively chased birds that trespassed on their territories.

It is noteworthy that males are not clearly dominant over females in every hummingbird species. One explanation for this is that males, of species in which males are dominant, show higher degrees of wing-disc loading and are therefore more able to maneuver and accelerate rapidly. These flight skills of male rufous hummingbirds, and of males of other species, may therefore allow the males to more effectively chase and intimidate intruders, or escape birds chasing them, than the less-agile females. Despite their lack of success at chasing away invading hummingbirds, female rufous hummingbirds are more able to keep their body masses up when food is scarce than are males.

PREDATION

North American hummingbirds are generally thought to not only have few predators but to not die in very large numbers from predation. There is still uncertainty, nonetheless, about the extent to which attacks on hummingbirds by predators, especially attacks that are not fatal, occur. Researchers have noted that many rufous hummingbirds in Arizona did not have any tertiary feathers, or retrices, and appeared to have survived predation. The researchers proposed that hummingbirds might be attacked more frequently than scientists had previously argued. There are, additionally, numerous observations in the literature of hummingbirds being attacked by birds, such as by a bicolored hawk, but not being killed or obviously wounded.

Although hummingbirds are not especially vulnerable to predation, numerous animals are known to prey upon hummingbirds. The bat falcon is one bird that does regularly prey on some hummingbirds, but hummingbirds are also attacked and eaten by a variety of birds. Hummingbirds at tropical latitudes are frequently attacked by the tiny hawk, and hummingbirds are also sometimes killed by the merlin, sharp-shinned hawk, and American kestrel. Other birds that have been observed killing or attacking hummingbirds are the Baltimore oriole, gray kingbird, brown-crested flycatcher, blue-crowned motmot, curve-billed thrasher, and roadrunner. One researcher also observed a white-necked puffbird killing and eating a hummingbird in Panama.

It is noteworthy that some of the predators, such as the tiny hawk, are not especially large. Some tiny hawks are roughly the sizes of robins, and this could suggest that their maneuverability makes them more able to catch quickly moving hummingbirds.

Hummingbirds are also at a low risk of being preyed upon by other animals. For example, hummingbirds can sometimes die after they are caught in

Danger can come from unexpected quarters; bullfrogs have been known to catch and eat hummingbirds in the wild.

spiderwebs. Since many hummingbirds rely heavily on spiders for protein, it is perhaps not surprising that small hummingbirds are especially vulnerable to this problem. Researchers have also reported that hummingbirds can be eaten by frogs, praying mantises, and, perhaps most surprisingly and atypically, bass. Hummingbirds may also be stung and killed by wasps, some spiders, such as the whip spider, or tailless whip scorpions.

Many more hummingbird deaths occur in nests. Most hummingbirds lay only between two and three eggs, and it is often the case that none of the birds in a nest survives to adulthood. An average of 54 percent of the time, all of the hummingbirds in a nest die either before or after they are hatched. When researchers look at the reasons for nest failure in different species of hummingbirds, it is clear that most of the deaths occur when predators eat the eggs or eat the nestling birds. A nestling bird is a bird that has not developed the feathers necessary for flight. A young bird that has flight feathers, that can fly, and that may or may not be spending time near the nest is a fledgling. About 59 percent of the deaths, in one study, resulted from the eating of eggs by predators, and about 25 percent of the deaths occurred when predators ate the nestling birds. In other cases, the young hummingbirds died because their mothers had abandoned the nest.

Avoiding Danger

Various lines of experimental and observational evidence suggest that hummingbirds routinely take measures to avoid predation. To safeguard their young, for example, they appear to choose inconspicuous locations for their nests. When researchers gave Anna's hummingbirds a choice between an artificial feeder with no flower and a feeder with a large, fanned-out, artifical flower, the feeding pattern of the birds changed. When the hummingbirds fed at the artificial flower, which interfered with their ability to see their surroundings, the birds fed intermittently, going in and out for a few seconds at a time. In contrast, the birds fed almost continuously at the feeder that did not interfere with their vision. Hummingbirds often pollinate tube-shaped flowers that do not interfere with the birds' peripheral vision. Such flowers are similar to the shape of the unobstructed feeder that the birds preferred in the experiments.

Researchers have also frequently observed hummingbirds scanning the areas around the flowers at which they are feeding. Hummingbirds tend to prefer to not feed extremely close to the ground, and researchers think this is a strategy to avoid predation. The attention that hummingbirds pay to would-be predators, therefore, may help explain the rarity with which hummingbirds are killed by predators. Consistent with this, scientists have noted that an Anna's hummingbird refused to feed from a feeder if any roadrunners were in the vicinity of the feeder.

Hummingbirds also evidently make special noises when they are being chased or when they have been caught. When a hummingbird had been

Energy Used in Chasing Hummingbirds and Insects

Before a hummingbird decides whether to chase either other hummingbirds or insects from its territory, it must decide if each effort is worth the energy expenditure. Researchers in Panama watched the territory of a rufous-tailed hummingbird, a species that has almost never been seen breeding in the United States and is not the same as a rufous hummingbird, and noted that the hummingbird chased 98 percent of the 599 hummingbirds that invaded its territory over a twelve-hour period. In contrast, the hummingbird only chased 131 of 236 large bees, or about 56 percent, that invaded its territory over the same twelve-hour period. This study highlights the enormous number of intrusions that a hummingbird living at tropical latitudes may have to deal with on a given day. Researchers additionally estimated that the amount of nectar produced on a given day within the hummingbird's territory was only three times the amount that the hummingbird needed to consume on a given day. A hummingbird's territory may thus not contain a large amount of excess, or "disposable," nectar. If the hummingbird had allowed the other hummingbirds to invade its territory without being chased, researchers think the nectar supply would have been rapidly depleted. Hummingbirds evidently choose nonetheless to less frequently chase invaders that are of very small sizes, such as bees and butterflies, than invaders, such as other hummingbirds, that are larger. Researchers noted that hummingbirds were more likely to chase large bees and hummingbirds that frequently invaded the birds' territories.

caught, for example, but had not yet been killed by a puffbird in Panama, a scientist reported that the bird made a shrill sound to express its distress. Hummingbirds are known to make similar sounds when they are fleeing from birds of prey.

TERRITORIALITY AND TRAPLINING

Many hummingbirds are not always able to establish rigidly defined, continuous territories, for various reasons. In some cases, this failure or "lack" of territoriality is specific to the females of a given species. In other cases, one species of hummingbird in a given area becomes more dominant than one or more other species. The less-dominant species may then be forced to get nectar and other food by invading other birds' territories or developing some other kind of feeding pattern. Researchers refer to any nonterritorial feeding approach of hummingbirds as traplining, but other researchers prefer to use more specific terms, such as robbing, to describe feeding approaches of non-territorial hummingbirds.

What Is a Trapline?

Hummingbirds that do not have territories often establish so-called "foraging circuits," also known as traplines. The word trapline is most commonly used to describe a circuitous path that connects traps set by a hunter. A traplining hummingbird follows the path along its foraging circuits, and each flower or group of flowers, separated from the next feeding site by a distance, is analogous to a hunter's trap. The flowers in an actual hummingbird territory may be either quite spread out or grouped in a relatively small, dense area. When hummingbirds feed by traplining, the flowers do tend to be more spread out than in a territory. But the circuitous and spread-out quality of a trapline is not really the key feature that distinguishes it from a territory. A trapline differs from a territory because the hummingbird does not defend the flowers along the trapline, sometimes because the flowers are part of another hummingbird's territory. A traplining hummingbird does keep some kind of mental map of the circuit, however, and tends to visit the flowers in the same order from day to day. When the nectar stores in the flowers along the trapline have become replenished, the hummingbird will "make the rounds" again, much as a hunter would, feed on the nectar, and then move along down the circuit.

Most, but not all, of the hummingbirds that trapline live throughout the year at tropical or subtropical latitudes. The magnificent and broad-tailed hummingbirds are two North American species that trapline significant amounts of the time, but any hummingbird that does not have a territory can be viewed as a trapliner. Some species, such as the rufous hummingbird, are very dominant and do not have to very frequently rely on traplining for nectar.

Researchers have found that the traplines of tropical hummingbirds, such as the long-tailed hermit hummingbird, are dynamic. A hummingbird will stop visiting a collection of flowers on a trapline if the flowers stop producing significant nectar. Hummingbirds, additionally, may have to trapline during periods when they cannot maintain territories. A species, for example, may become temporarily subordinate to other species in a given area and have to trapline. Traplining can therefore be a kind of flexible stopgap measure, even though it may be used relatively frequently by some species. Different species of hermit hummingbirds, for example, tend to rely heavily on traplining. Researchers have noted that an individual hermit was often the only hummingbird, or one of just a handful, that fed from some plants on its trapline. Hummingbirds may thus be able to have somewhat exclusive access to some plants that they feed from via traplining.

Large Hummingbirds Trapline Too

The magnificent hummingbird is one North American species that is known to frequently use traplining to get nectar. Because many of the magnificents that breed in the United States do not set up feeding territories, they have to trapline; but some magnificents do set up territories. Magnificents are, on average, second only to the blue-throated hummingbirds in size among species that breed in the United States. Does the large size of the magnificent somehow impair its ability to easily and skillfully chase invaders? It is not clear. Researchers have also found that the blue-throated hummingbird sometimes traplines, even though it is usually capable in the United States of dominating all other species in territorial encounters. Both rufous and other small hummingbirds are thought to be able to use their small sizes to their advantage by changing directions and accelerating rapidly in chasing away larger intruders and thereby maintaining their territories. But magnificents that live throughout the year in Mexico are frequently able to maintain feeding territories, so their size there would seem to not be a major factor in causing them to trapline. Magnificents are generally a very unusual species and, in spite of the dominant quality of their traplining, eat more insects than other species.

The planalto hermit is one of many hermit species that use a trapline—a circuit of regularly visited food sources that doesn't necessarily correspond to the bird's home territory.

Magnificents, like various species of hermit hummingbirds, tend to be more dominant as high-reward trapliners—hummingbirds that do not set up a territory and tend to be able to successfully impinge upon other hummingbirds' territories. The high-reward trapliner tends thus to be a large hummingbird with a long bill that may be dominant with respect to some of the territorial hummingbirds in the same area. Low-reward trapliners, in contrast, tend to have smaller bodies and sneak nectar from other hummingbirds' territories. These trapliners tend to be at a lower point in the hierarchy and can frequently also be described as robbers or filchers, as discussed later in this chapter.

Adapted for Traplining?

Traplining hummingbirds, according to the traditional argument, are physically adapted to hover and fly more efficiently than do territorial hummingbirds. The explanation for this has been that hummingbirds with shorter wings, which increase wing-disc loading and tend to be characteristic of territorial hummingbirds, are more able to maneuver aggressively and chase invaders across short distances. In this context of territorial defense or lack thereof, efficient flight means metabolically efficient flight. A species that has to thus rely on traplining will tend to have lower wing-disc loading and be able to fly efficiently over longer distances. But trapliners will not be able to "efficiently" use bursts of energy and aggression to chase invaders.

Some researchers have noted, however, that hummingbirds cannot necessarily be labeled as either traplining or territorial hummingbirds. One North American species that tends to sometimes have territories but to rely on traplining the rest of the time is the broad-tailed hummingbird. Because of this tendency, the broad-tailed is sometimes described as a facultative trapliner. Something that is facultative can occur under certain conditions but is not obligatory. These and other hummingbirds appear to be flexible in adjusting their foraging strategies in ways that take advantage of their individual physical differences.

TERRITORIAL ZONES AND PERIPHERAL FORAGING

Some North American hummingbirds, such as rufous hummingbirds, tend to feed around the peripheries of their territories mostly in the early morning—the core behavior of peripheral foraging. Hummingbirds that engage in peripheral foraging tend not to concentrate on any one portion of their territories in the middle of the day. In the evening, however, these hummingbirds tend to feed from flowers in the central portions of their territories. So there is an overall movement, as the day progresses, from the periphery to the interior of the territory.

Some other species, such as the Anna's hummingbird, have a core territory, also known as a primary territory, and a larger, spread-out secondary territory. The secondary territory is also known as a "buffer zone" and is only really part of the territory during the breeding months. Researchers have noted that the primary territories of Anna's hummingbirds tend to be 0.25 acre, and the primary and secondary zones together are sometimes between 6 and 10 acres. This seasonal change in the defensive perimeter is not the same as peripheral foraging, which involves a change in the feeding pattern over the course of a day, but it is helpful to see the ways different species of hummingbirds maintain mental maps of different sections of their territories.

Extraterritorial Feeding
Rufous hummingbirds are not the only North American species that uses peripheral foraging or similar feeding approaches. Researchers have observed blue-throated hummingbirds in Texas feeding on nectar from plants in an area surrounding their territories in the mornings. These hummingbirds feed in these "extraterritorial" areas in the mornings for up to twenty minutes at a time and end up being in these areas for up to 16 percent of the day. This behavior was not specifically studied in the context of peripheral foraging, but the morning feeding, in an area that surrounds the primary territory, is generally consistent with peripheral foraging. The explanation for this behavior is similar to but not the same as the explanation for peripheral foraging. Essentially, the blue-throateds were dominant, by virtue of their large bodies, over all the other species and could afford, particularly in the mornings when the amounts of nectar are highest in almost all plants, to risk leaving their territories undefended. It is also possible that these extraterritorial areas were essentially secondary territories and that this behavior was, in fact, a type of peripheral foraging.

Researchers think that peripheral foraging helps rufous hummingbirds and other species that are not as large as the blue-throateds reduce the amounts of nectar that are lost from flowers by intruding birds. Although it seems clear that this behavior is advantageous, researchers are not immediately able to offer a clear explanation for the behavior. This is because in the absence of any birds invading the territory, it is energetically wasteful from the standpoint of physical exertion for a hummingbird to fly back and forth around one section, such as the periphery, of its territory.

Morning Activity
That the amounts of nectar in flowers tend to be the greatest in the morning hours helps to provide a notable bioenergetic explanation for peripheral foraging. The hummingbird defending its territory and the would-be invaders all know that the nectar levels are highest in the morning. At the same time the hummingbird feeds on abundant nectar sources along the periphery of its territory in the morning, it also prevents other birds from taking parts of those

nectar reserves. Researchers have also found that hummingbirds are able to send a strong message, as it were, to morning intruders by vigorously defending the peripheries of their territories. A hummingbird that is lax in chasing away other birds early in the day can send the message that its territory is essentially open for business to any birds that would impinge upon it during the entire day. The hummingbird thus needs to chase away invaders during the hours of peak nectar availability.

Hummingbirds that engage in peripheral foraging also try to feed on flowers that invaders have recently attempted to steal nectar from. Given that invaders tend to feed on flowers near the periphery of a territory, this strategy is, to some extent, simply part of the more general strategy by the defending hummingbird of feeding along the periphery of the territory. But feeding on recently invaded territory immediately after chasing the invaders away allows a territorial hummingbird to forage along strategically chosen parts of the periphery. This adds another layer of complexity to the feeding habits of rufous hummingbirds and members of other species.

Hummingbirds are even able to use these complex strategies when feeding from stopover territories, which are the temporary territories that the birds set up during migration. Rufous hummingbirds, for example, are able to set up stopover territories or habitats within a few days and then shift the boundaries of their territories in a dynamic and flexible manner. When

Studies show that the rufous hummingbird feeds at the flowers around the edges of its territory first thing in the day; this morning "peripheral foraging" is part of the complex feeding strategy hummingbirds employ to thrive in the wild.

Territorial Hummingbirds
and Crop Filling

Territorial hummingbirds often eat smaller meals than do hummingbirds that are unable to maintain territories. Researchers have essentially found that male Anna's hummingbirds that do not have territories generally feed, during an intrusion into another hummingbird's territory, for as long as possible. These feedings often completely fill their crops. Researchers think that this strategy helps the birds to minimize the number of intrusions they have to make into other birds' territories. Scientists note that a hummingbird will sometimes eat as much as 10 percent of its daily caloric intake in one visit to a hummingbird feeder. The large crops of hummingbirds thus allow them considerable flexibility in their feeding strategies.

Territorial hummingbirds, in contrast, generally consume smaller and more frequent meals. Anna's hummingbirds that had established territories, for example, were found to consume less than one-third of the mass of nectar, in a typical feeding, as did intruders. Whereas intruders sometimes fed for ninety or more seconds at a time, the same feeding for territorial hummingbirds usually lasted sixteen to nineteen seconds. A territorial hummingbird has to make sure its body weight does not increase too much because the extra mass of food, stored in the crop, can considerably decrease the agility with which a hummingbird can chase other birds from its territory. If an intruder invades a territory and becomes sluggish after a big meal, the hummingbird only has to fly a short distance out of the territory and wait for its crop to empty. Although a territorial hummingbird has to be constantly alert, it often eats large meals at the end of the day because sleep is near and the need to chase away invaders less likely.

the nectar supplies become depleted from a given portion of their territories, they are able to leave behind that portion of territory and still apply, in an ongoing fashion, their complex, peripheral foraging strategies. Bad weather sometimes severely damages flowers and forces hummingbirds to adjust their territorial boundaries. In other cases, hummingbirds are forced to abandon parts of the territory that have been depleted of nectar by invaders or by the birds themselves. Especially on the periphery of a territory, however, it can be difficult for a hummingbird to always be aware of the specific flowers that have been fed upon by invaders. If a territorial hummingbird only has a mental map of the flowers that it has fed from and drained of nectar, then the

Intruders to Territories in the Tropics and Temperate Locations

Various similarities and differences exist in the territories—and the behaviors involved in defending those territories—of tropical and temperate hummingbirds. Researchers monitored the territory of a rufous-tailed hummingbird for intruders and found that very large numbers of them attempted to feed from the territory. Over a twelve-hour period, researchers found that an average of forty-nine hummingbirds and eleven large bees per hour invaded the territory and attempted to feed. Even more remarkably, this tropical territory was only 344 square feet in area, a very tiny area. In contrast, rufous hummingbirds, setting up temporary, stopover territories in the Sierra Nevada of California, had much larger territories and many fewer intrusions. These hummingbirds had territories between 1,076 and 19,375 square feet in size and had to deal with only four to five intrusions per hour. These comparisons highlight the extreme density of life in the tropics and the adaptations that hummingbirds, living in either the tropics or temperate latitudes, are able to make.

The tropical and temperate hummingbirds did not spend drastically different amounts of time on any one activity. The rufous hummingbirds discussed above, for example, spent an average of 2.3 percent of their time chasing, 74 percent of their time perching and preening, and 17 to 25 percent of their time feeding. Despite having to deal with up to ten times as many intrusions as the temperate hummingbirds, the tropical hummingbird, discussed above, spent 11 percent of its time chasing, 57 percent of its time perching, and 18 percent of its time feeding. This makes sense, given the small size of the tropical hummingbird's territory. But it is telling that hummingbirds are able to adjust the dimensions of their territories in ways that let them effectively budget their time.

bird is likely to waste energy in trying to visit flowers that have been fed upon by some other bird. Peripheral foraging can thus help increase the accuracy of a hummingbird's mental map of its territory and allow it to shift the boundaries of its territory in the most appropriate ways.

Impact of Weight Gain
The tendency of territorial hummingbirds to feed near the centers of their territories as the day progresses is not just driven by changes in the behavior

of intruders. Researchers think that rufous hummingbirds, to some extent, move toward the central portions of their territories because of weight gain throughout the day. Hummingbirds generally weigh more at the end of the day than at the beginning, either because of an increase in food or water mass in the body (humans also tend to weigh more at the end of the day than at the beginning). The birds thus do not have to expend as much energy in feeding around the centers of their territories, given that the distance between flowers tends to be lower there. Researchers have found that the flowers near the centers of rufous hummingbirds' territories tend to be more densely packed. But the decision to feed near the center, late in the day, can also be explained in terms of geometric principles. A hummingbird will have to expend more energy to zigzag between flowers that are on opposite edges of its territory, along the periphery, than to zigzag within a smaller area.

COMPETITIVE ENCOUNTERS

Some hummingbirds use specific feeding strategies that can be regarded as either types of traplining or as behaviors that are in between traplining and territoriality, but any hummingbird that does not have a feeding territory at a given time can be regarded as a trapliner. A traplining hummingbird, such as the magnificent hummingbird, tends to set up the trapline in a way that does not produce very many competitive encounters with other hummingbirds. In many cases, however, traplining hummingbirds have to interact with other hummingbirds. Researchers refer to nonterritorial hummingbirds that interact with other hummingbirds in specific ways as filchers or robbers, challengers, marauders, generalists, and piercers or nectar robbers. Marauding, thus, is essentially high-reward traplining that involves a territorial conflict, and robbing is basically low-reward traplining that includes a territorial invasion.

Researchers have classified the Koepke's hermit hummingbird as a high-reward trapliner and generalist, meaning the species does not usually set up territories and is often, but not always, dominant when its traplining brings it in contact with other hummingbirds. The broad-tailed hummingbird, as a facultative trapliner, is one species that tends to use some of the strategies discussed in this section. But any hummingbird that does not have a territory will probably use one or more of these approaches at different times. Most of the terms discussed in this section describe different approaches to the invasion of a territory, although nectar robbing does not always involve invasion. Researchers sometimes use the various terms loosely, but it is possible to bring some clarity to the picture.

Dominating Marauders

Marauders are actually dominant to the territorial hummingbird and tend to be members of a species that is larger than the territorial hummingbird. A marauder thus takes what it wants. True marauding, in which a hummingbird is much larger than another and is capable of freely intruding upon the

The interaction of hummingbirds often features aggressive encounters that serve a variety of purposes. Here, two male Anna's hummingbirds face off.

other bird's territory, is probably most likely to occur between members of two tropical species. Different species of North American, temperate hummingbirds do not as drastically differ from one another in size as do different species of tropical hummingbirds. One behavior that is generally consistent with marauding is the high-reward traplining of the magnificent hummingbird within the United States. This large species is likely to dominate hummingbirds that get in the way of its traplining.

Subordinate Filchers

The term filching is sometimes used to describe the intruding behavior of a hummingbird that is in a relatively fixed, subordinate role to the territory's owner. A very small species of hummingbird, for example, might always be at a disadvantage, because of its size, to members of other, more consistently territorial species. Researchers very rarely use the term filching in the scientific literature and more often refer to submissive invaders as robbers or even nectar robbers. A true nectar robber feeds on a flower by destroying or damaging the nectar-producing parts of the flower and does not pollinate the flower. Invading that is done secretively and does not involve true nectar robbing should probably thus be, for the sake of clarity, referred to as robbing. The key point is that a robber forages by sneaking onto the territory and does not challenge the territorial hummingbird. As discussed below, robbers tend to be female.

A challenger, in contrast, is a hummingbird that invades a territory in a very brazen and aggressive manner. A challenger does not necessarily have the inherent size advantage over the territorial hummingbird as does a marauder. This fact helps distinguish challenging from marauding. That a challenger is invading with the intent of taking over part or all of the territory is the additional implication.

Challenging versus Robbing
Certain types of hummingbirds tend to invade territories as either robbers or challengers. Consistent with their submissive behavior and secretive intrusions, robbers are often female or younger male hummingbirds. Although some challengers may be female, most adult male hummingbirds that invade territories are challengers. Not all challengers are thus necessarily male, but most male invaders behave in a challenging manner. Researchers have noted that males essentially cannot be good robbers. An adult male that tries to invade in a secretive manner will usually be noticed and chased away, as a result of either its relatively large size or intense, iridescent colors. An adult male that wants to feed during its invasion will therefore often be forced to confront, or challenge, the territorial hummingbird. Female hummingbirds and younger hummingbirds, in contrast, are robbers because they can be.

Some hummingbirds that invade territories behave in either dominant or submissive ways, depending on the circumstances. A hummingbird might invade the territory of one hummingbird, for example, and then chase another invader off the territory. Hummingbirds that have to rely on this mixed approach are still nonterritorial and can be regarded as trapliners. The hummingbird might then be chased off by the territorial owner. The hummingbird, acting in a subordinate role, can therefore be chased, and also be a chaser, acting in a dominant role. Some researchers have referred to a hummingbird in this sort of position as a generalist, but this term is potentially confusing. The term "generalist" is also used to describe a hummingbird that feeds from a wide range of flowers and does not specialize in feeding from a narrow range of plants. The same word is thus used to describe separate behaviors.

Some hummingbirds are true nectar robbers or piercers. In true nectar robbing, a hummingbird pierces a part of the flower, usually the base, that

does not contain the structures involved in pollination. A primary nectar robber is a hummingbird or other bird or insect that takes the first meal by piercing the flower. A hummingbird will sometimes act as a secondary nectar
robber by robbing nectar from the base of a flower that has already been
opened up by another bird or insect. In other cases, a hummingbird may
feed from flowers that are usually pollinated by insects or bats. Finally, some
hummingbirds are able to obtain nectar without serving as a pollinator by
sneaking their bills in between the flower petals of plants that have certain
types of petals. In all these cases, the hummingbird generally does not pollinate the plant and may damage the capacity of the plant to reproduce and
supply nectar to other hummingbirds. Some hummingbird species have serrations on their bills that help them with nectar robbing. Other hummingbirds obtain some of their nectar by nectar robbing and the rest by the usual
way. The white-eared and berylline hummingbirds, for example, are North
American species that are known to rely on nectar robbing some of the time.
Although nectar robbing does not necessarily involve any direct interaction
between two hummingbirds, the behavior indirectly affects the ways other
hummingbirds feed and is therefore similar to passive aggression.

Although nectar robbing may seem purely destructive, researchers have
noted that the behavior can sometimes indirectly improve the pollination
and reproduction of flowering plants. A nectar-robbing hummingbird, for
example, can eat all the nectar from, or damage the flowers on, a plant and
force other hummingbirds to expand their territories. If other hummingbirds
have to fly farther between plants because of nectar robbers, this can help a
plant spread its pollen across a larger area of land.

Mobbing

Hummingbirds also will sometimes recognize a predator, such as an owl, and
"mob" it in an attempt to chase away or intimidate the predator. Some of
these so-called "mobbings" occur when groups of hummingbirds simultaneously fly near a predatory bird and threaten it. In other cases, researchers
have observed hummingbirds threatening owls, for example, individually
but in response to the threatening flight of another hummingbird. Scientists
sometimes refer to this as a "contagious" behavior, or a secondary response,
with the actions of one bird encouraging others to perhaps be more bold and
act in a similar manner. There is evidence that hummingbirds mob a variety
of animals in the wild, including owls, hawks, jays, and even cats and snakes.

The mobbing behaviors of hummingbirds can be surprisingly aggressive
in comparison with the mobbings by other birds. Researchers observed
Anna's hummingbirds fly toward the eyes of a stuffed owl repeatedly, then
fly away. Although this experiment was performed with a dead, stuffed owl,
the hummingbirds treated the owl as a live, potential predator. These hummingbirds flew within 2 inches of the eyes and head of the owl, making
pecking or piercing movements, without actually touching the owl. The

hummingbirds also made shrill noises, at a constant pitch, when they attacked the owl.

Hummingbirds tend to attack a variety of different owls and attack more aggressively at certain times during the year. Costa's hummingbirds and Anna's hummingbirds attacked short-eared owls, screech-owls, and pygmy-owls. The Anna's hummingbird, however, tends to attack screech-owls mainly during the breeding and nesting season and mainly after having previously seen another hummingbird attacking the owl. The peak for all mobbing behaviors, in hummingbirds and other birds, has been shown to span the interval between March and June. This interval roughly corresponds to the breeding and nesting season. The numbers of mobbing attacks decrease almost to zero during other months. There is also a small increase in December and January, perhaps because birds are moving toward or into their springtime territories and establishing themselves. The reason for this winter increase is not especially clear, however.

POLLINATION

Hummingbirds carry pollen from flower to flower on various parts of their bodies. Grains of pollen are present on the anthers of a flower. As a hummingbird feeds on nectar from a flower of a certain species, pollen grains brush off onto the hummingbird's head or jaw. When the hummingbird feeds on nectar from another flower of that species, some of the pollen grains can rub or fall off onto the stigmas of the flower. The stigmas, receptors for pollen, are associated with the "female" part of the flower.

Pollinated Flowers

Hummingbirds pollinate flowers that tend to have some characteristics in common with one another. Most of the flowers from which hummingbirds eat nectar do not produce strong smells. Since hummingbirds do not themselves appear to have strong senses of smell, researchers think that there was probably no evolutionary, or reproductive, advantage for the plants they pollinate to produce fragrances. Such plants would have gradually lost their scent.

Hummingbirds also tend to feed from flowers that are red or dark orange, although not all of the flowers that hummingbirds feed from are red or orange. Hummingbirds have frequently been observed trying to feed from red objects or parts of objects, such as red car taillights, but the color red is not really the most important factor that draws a hummingbird to a source of nectar. In some cases, the hummingbirds that were trying to feed from red objects were known to be young or extremely hungry. Instead, hummingbirds more strongly prefer flowers that are physically accessible to them. If a hummingbird cannot hover and feed from a red flower without hitting a tree, for example, the hummingbird will probably prefer to feed from a blue flower. Similarly, hummingbirds generally prefer nectar that does not have

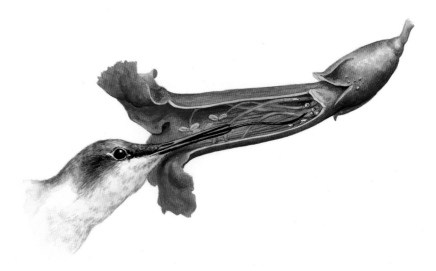

Hummingbirds take nectar from a variety of sources, but researchers note a tendency to choose red or dark orange flowers that have a tube-shaped base and flared ends. As the bird feeds, it extends its tongue into nectar-rich spots, often getting a dusting of pollen on its face and body in the process.

too high of a sucrose concentration. A hummingbird generally prefers to eat good nectar from a flower that is blue, or a color other than red, than to eat poor-quality nectar from a red flower.

The bases of the flowers that hummingbirds eat from and pollinate also tend to be tube shaped. The petals of these flowers may, nonetheless, fan out at the ends. Flowers with this shape may deposit more pollen onto the faces and bodies of hummingbirds as the hummingbirds insert their bills to obtain nectar than flowers that are more shallow and bowl shaped. Tube-shaped flowers, moreover, may prevent bees and other insects from taking nectar from the flower. A plant may, for example, have evolved to take advantage of pollination by hummingbirds in particular. If the plant's flowers allow bees to deplete the nectar and also to act as poor pollinators, then the plant will be at a reproductive disadvantage.

The open parts of flowers that hummingbirds feed from are also often directed downward, or at least not upward. It is apparent that this would be advantageous for hummingbirds, given that a hummingbird would have to hover in an awkward position to obtain nectar from a flower facing upward. Although hummingbirds do feed from some flowers that do not provide them with a "horizontal" point of access to nectar, it is possible that the downward hanging of a flower helps to discourage butterflies or other insects from pollinating the flower. It is known that butterflies require some sort of perch on the flower in order to obtain nectar from it. Researchers have observed hummingbirds sitting on a branch or other perch while they eat nectar from flowers, but hummingbirds generally have to be in hovering flight to obtain their nectar. The hummingbird moth, nonetheless, is an example of an insect that is able to obtain nectar from flowers that hummingbirds feed from while it hovers. Hovering does not thus always allow hummingbirds exclusive access to their flowers of choice.

Hummingbirds also mainly pollinate perennial plants, which are plants that survive in the ground for a number of winters. The association of hummingbirds and perennial plants may have been partially driven by the coevolution of plants with hummingbirds. Hummingbirds have very good memories and often migrate along the same paths from year to year. A collection of perennial plants may thus be visited by the same hummingbirds in multiple years.

The plants that hummingbirds pollinate also often have large flowers that bloom for fairly long periods of time. This feature helps distinguish the flowers that hummingbirds pollinate from those that insects pollinate. Researchers have noted that a plant must expend more energy to make large flowers than to make small flowers, and this might appear to put plants with large flowers at a reproductive disadvantage. It is noteworthy, however, that hummingbirds are physically less fragile than many insects and can therefore serve as pollinators during a rainfall or windstorm. Additionally, the activity level of a hummingbird is less likely to be affected by fluctuations in temperature. Many insects are not as active during cold weather as they are on a hot day. There are, thus, always evolutionary trade-offs when a plant has become adapted to take advantage of a particular pollinator.

There is other evidence that the plants that hummingbirds visit have become adapted to provide nourishment across a broad temperature range. Insects pollinate plants that tend to produce nectar that contains around 40 percent sucrose and other sugars; nectar that is so highly concentrated with sugars tends to also be viscous. The viscosity of nectar also increases as the temperature cools. Hummingbirds generally consume nectar in the wild that is about 20 to 25 percent sucrose. It is thus possible that the nectar with lower sucrose concentrations is especially low in viscosity and therefore especially edible to hummingbirds at lower temperatures and across a wider range of temperatures. Alternatively, some researchers have suggested that lower sugar concentrations in nectar force hummingbirds to visit a flower more times on a given day in order to get a given amount of nourishment. An increase in the numbers of visits to each flower might be expected to increase the amount of pollen that would be deposited on a hummingbird, and this would provide the plant with a reproductive advantage.

BATHING AND GROOMING
Hummingbirds frequently bathe or wash themselves in water. The long-tailed hermit hummingbird, for example, a hummingbird that lives and

A male Anna's hummingbird bathes in splashing water—regular cleaning and preening are essential to any bird's survival.

breeds at tropical latitudes in Central America, will hover above a stream and then descend part of the way into the water. Subsequently, these hummingbirds often perch on a branch and shake the water from their bodies vigorously, causing their whole bodies to vibrate in what scientists have described as a "blur." In other cases, hummingbirds fly and shake their bodies in a rainfall, a waterfall, or even a lawn sprinkler.

Researchers and other people have noted that hummingbirds also routinely fly during rainfalls and clean themselves in mists or small water droplets. Some bird enthusiasts, for example, have pointed modified hoses at trees and observed hummingbirds cleaning themselves under or next to leaves as the water drips or splashes in and around the leaves. Hummingbirds have also been observed bathing or fluttering their wings under leaves that had already been covered with water from a rainfall. It is also noteworthy that hummingbirds evidently fly around during rainfalls more consistently than other birds do. It is not clear what the reason for this is.

Hummingbids also spend a fair amount of time grooming, or preening, their feathers. Hummingbirds have a secretory gland that produces an oil onto the skin of their tails. Hummingbirds use some of this oil to smooth out and lubricate their feathers with their bills. This oil also prevents fungal and bacterial overgrowth of hummingbird wings. Hummingbirds also sometimes use their feet to remove nectar or other materials, such as tree sap, from their faces.

4

The Annual Cycle

NESTING SEASON

The courtship process among hummingbirds can be complex and, at certain stages, difficult to tell apart from behaviors related to territorial defense. Male and female hummingbirds do not generally bond with or help each other after mating. Despite the cold, unromantic quality of the interactions between the hummingbird sexes, the processes surrounding courtship, mating, and nesting are frequently intricate and subtle.

Female hummingbirds make their nests before they court and mate. Females do sometimes add on to their nests after they have mated and laid their eggs, but the gestation process physiologically drains a hummingbird. Females have frequently been observed laying their eggs in relatively flat nests—unlike the cup-shaped nests one normally expects to see. The gestation period for hummingbirds is also very short, so a female that has just mated would probably not have enough time, before laying her eggs, to build even this type of partial nest from scratch.

Many hummingbirds produce two sets, or broods, of offspring and two nests during each summer breeding season. Black-chinned hummingbirds in New Mexico and Arizona, for example, begin their first nest in the middle of April and leave that nest by the end of June. The same birds then set up a second nest by early July and leave the second nest by early September. Often, female black-chinned hummingbirds will begin building the second nest while they are still feeding their first brood at the first nest. Violet-crowned hummingbirds and broad-billed hummingbirds also nest, in the Southwest, during roughly the same period as do the black-chinned hummingbirds.

Nest Heights

Different species of hummingbirds are known to nest at different distances from the ground, but sometimes the range of heights is large within a given species. In the Southwest, black-chinned and violet-crowned hummingbirds generally nest in trees about 16 to 19 feet above the ground and do not

Courtship rituals between hummingbird pairs, such as this interaction between two blue-crowned woodnymphs, occur after the female builds a nest. Hummingbird pairs do not remain together after mating.

require dense forests for nesting. In the same area, Costa's hummingbirds have been found to nest in smaller trees as low as 3 to 7 feet off the ground. Although both black-chinned and violet-crowned hummingbirds are known to build nests in Arizona sycamore trees, violet-crowned hummingbirds tend to prefer nesting near the outer branches of the trees. In contrast, black-chinned hummingbirds are willing to nest anywhere in the trees, even near the trunks.

The trees that hummingbirds choose for nesting are sometimes in the open and not surrounded by many other trees. Researchers have noted, however, that a variety of different hummingbirds appear to nest near a rock face or in a tree surrounded by some other bushes. These choices of nesting sites may provide the birds with some shelter and prevent heat loss. Although the nests can sometimes be far from other trees and other hummingbirds' nests, it has been noted that rufous hummingbirds may build their nests very close to other nests. They will sometimes nest in groups of up to twenty nests, for example, with any one nest separated from another by only several feet.

Hummingbirds also may carefully choose the heights of their nests to avoid excessive wind or predators. Anna's hummingbirds in California have been observed creating nests in locations that are remarkably well shielded from wind gusts on, for example, three sides of the nests. They also often scout locations for days ahead of building their nests. In New Mexico and Arizona, researchers found that the higher the nests of black-chinned and violet-crowned hummingbirds were built, the more likely the nestlings were to be killed by other birds preying on them. Some species of hummingbirds nonetheless build nests as high as 70 feet off the ground, although the normal range tends to be 3 to 20 feet off the ground.

Quick Builders

Hummingbirds often build their nests within a few days and work fairly steadily to create them. A representative Anna's hummingbird, for example, worked for about nine days on its nest, although it disappeared from the nest-building site on some of those days. Researchers also have observed the violet-headed hummingbird, in Central America, leave its unfinished nest for a day or more at a time. Before hummingbirds actually finish their nests and lay their eggs, they do not necessarily behave as if they are guarding their nests carefully.

Hummingbirds use a variety of locally available materials to construct their nests. Hummingbirds in subtropical or temperate climates typically use tree twigs, packed densely in a small cup, to create their nests. The nest tends to only be between 1.5 and 2 inches in diameter and about 1 inch in depth. Other building materials include grass, moss, cocoons, and pinecones or pine needles. When hummingbirds nest in suburban or semiurban environments,

Nesting and Nectar Supply

The times at which hummingbirds nest appear to agree remarkably well with the peaks in local nectar production. In Guadalupe Canyon, for example, which extends through the southern portions of New Mexico and Arizona, the first peak in nectar availability from plants occurs between the end of April and the middle of June. This is the same period during which most of this area's hummingbirds, members of four species, set up their first nests. Plants do not produce very much nectar in the middle of June, but there is a local, second peak of nectar availability that lasts from the end of June until the beginning of September. This period is roughly the same time at which hummingbirds set up their second nests.

Hummingbird nests are tiny—as small as 2 inches in diameter for North American species—and are often held together by spiderwebs. Females usually lay two eggs just a few days after mating.

the birds may use soft trash, such as bits of paper towels, lint, string, or fabric from discarded clothing.

Many hummingbirds, including temperate hummingbirds, rely heavily on spiderwebs to act as a binding material for their nests. Hummingbirds use spiderwebs to bind leaves and twigs together, giving the nest a cemented-together look and quality, and also to attach the nest to branches or to other structures. It is noteworthy that hummingbirds kept in captivity or semi-captivity also depend heavily on spiderwebs to construct their nests. When hummingbirds do not have access to spiderwebs that are being actively maintained by living spiders, the birds may have difficulty making well-constructed nests.

Hummingbird nests are very intricate and generally very small. The nests of temperate hummingbirds are often as small as 2 inches in diameter and are hemispherically shaped, like a small cup. Some of the large, tropical hummingbirds make larger nests, as would be expected. Although hummingbird nests have been shown to vary a certain amount from species to species, and even within a given species, the nests all tend to be quite compact and fairly rigidly built.

Nests and Nectar

Scientists sometimes find that hummingbirds' nests are more abundant in areas in which the availability of nectar is also consistent and abundant. Hummingbirds attempt to nest in areas with abundant nectar-producing flowers, but these sources of nectar may become depleted in the vicinity of the nests at different times during a nesting period.

Female hummingbirds also generally defend their nests vigorously and may establish nesting territories, which are areas of land around the nest. Around the nest, females engage in defensive behaviors, such as chasing, against all male and female hummingbirds as well as animals and birds that are not hummingbirds. A nesting territory may or may not also be a feeding territory, depending on the types of plants that are growing around the nesting site. In some cases, the nesting territory may simply consist of the tree on which the female has built the nest. Females of different North American species also establish feeding territories that are not around nests, but nesting

Advantages of Sheltered Nests

Hummingbirds may have more than one motivation for often creating their nests in sheltered locations. Researchers cannot say if hummingbirds choose sheltered locations because they want to avoid predators, but hummingbirds do tend to build nests under rock shelves, along cliff walls, or in other sheltered locations in forests. Such locations also may help prevent excessive heat loss at night or in cold weather, particularly at nests in the northernmost latitudes at which hummingbirds breed.

Rufous hummingbirds in British Columbia, for example, tend to create nests at different heights and in different sorts of trees as the temperatures warm. These choices probably help the birds maintain their nests at temperatures that are slightly warmer than the surrounding air. The broad-tailed hummingbird is known to frequently nest in a small branch of a tree that is just underneath a second, larger branch. The larger branch tends to shelter the nest and may, as scientists suspect, help limit the loss of radiant heat. Based on temperature measurements of broad-tailed hummingbirds in their nests, researchers estimate that the absence of shelter provided by a branch may triple the level of radiant heat loss from the nest. These hummingbirds also bolster the weights and diameters of their nests as the nesting period progresses. Researchers think this nest growth also limits heat loss from the nest and any eggs or nestling birds inside it.

females cannot hold feeding territories that are distant from their nesting sites. Typically, they "commute" away from the nest in short trips and feed. In the most general sense, this is feeding by traplining.

TYPICAL COURTSHIP BEHAVIORS

Male and female hummingbirds generally only interact, for purposes other than chasing one another out of their territories, for the few days that are required to mate. Researchers have only very rarely reported male hummingbirds of North American species feeding females in or around a nest. Female hummingbirds generally do not create more than one set of offspring with any one male. A male and a female typically court each other for a few days and then mate for a few days after that; these are the only times during which they consistently interact on the same land area.

Female Testing

The courtship process begins for many species of North American hummingbirds with a female trespassing into the territory of a male. Females may be more likely to mate with males that have good quality territories, but the way in which females evaluate the quality of a territory is not entirely clear. There is some evidence that females "test" males by perching within their territories—female intruders are more likely than male intruders to perch within a male's territory. By perching and causing males to make a defensive flight display, the female may be able to evaluate the frequency and vigor with which the males display themselves. In the case of calliope hummingbirds breeding in British Columbia, researchers found that males with higher nectar intakes made more frequent displays. Although a male that makes frequent dive displays or buzzing shuttle displays is likely to be more well fed and have a higher quality territory, the displays may be the factor that females look for. Researchers have noted that these initial flight displays in response to an intrusion by a female can therefore have a dual role and be used in both defense and courtship. There is also evidence, however, that females intrude on males' territories simply to eat nectar and then remain for mating in territories that provide abundant nectar.

Hummingbirds generally mate while the female is perched on a branch or other site. In some cases, the male will hover and mate with a perched female. The male hummingbird hovers behind the female and then mates from behind for an extremely brief period of time. There have been some reports suggesting that broad-tailed or violet-crowned hummingbirds mate in flight, but most of the evidence indicates that hummingbirds do not actually mate this way.

Lekking

Male hummingbirds of some tropical species, particularly species of hermit hummingbirds in the genus *Phaethornis*, as well as some North American

Hybrid Hummingbirds

Scientists have found many examples of hybrid hummingbirds. This interspecies mating has sometimes been, albeit loosely, attributed to the general promiscuity of hummingbird mating practices. Researchers have been identifying, collecting, and reporting on hybrid hummingbirds for the better part of a hundred years. The process of confirming the two parent species of a hybrid can sometimes be controversial and challenging.

It is not clear how common hybridization is among hummingbirds, but hybrids of North American species have been identified. Given the low diversity of species that actually breed in North America, these hybrids of temperate species are, at the very least, interesting. A hybrid of a broad-tailed hummingbird and a white-eared hummingbird that was found in Arizona is an example of an intergeneric hybrid, meaning that the two parents are not even members of the same genus. A genus of hummingbird species usually contains between one and nine species, with many genera including one or two species. Although hybrids involving North American species are probably rare, members of the two known species of bee hummingbirds, which live and breed in the tropics, are known to sometimes mate across species lines. This would be an example of intrageneric hybridization, meaning that the two parents are genetically very similar and members of species contained within the same genus.

species attempt to mate by congregating in leks—portions of land on which males compete for access to females. Lekking males make different songs and may engage in combative interactions with one another. Typically, only a few males will succeed in mating, and the males that succeed may mate with multiple females. The most general thing that sets lekking apart from normal courtship practices is that the courtship does not occur on a feeding territory and revolve around food or, more specifically, the quality of a feeding territory. Male hummingbirds that lek will defend their lek territories, or breeding territories, even though the territories do not contain nectar. The males feed from plants outside their breeding territories. The other main features of lekking are that the males tend to rely heavily on complex vocalizations or songs, not only with females but with other males, but do not necessarily do individual dive displays for the females.

Some North American hummingbirds engage in mating approaches that amount to lekking and occur in so-called "exploded leks." In a study in

Hermit hummingbirds, such as the saw-billed hermit, are well known for gathering in leks, areas where males battle each other for access to females. Other hummingbirds engage in "lekking" as well, including some North American species.

British Columbia, female calliope hummingbirds did not really enter males' territories to evaluate nectar availability and then use that information to decide to mate or not. The females mated instead with the males when there was no nectar to be eaten in what seemed more like pure mating grounds than feeding territories that the females could evaluate. In this sense, the males' territories were collectively like a lek that had been spread out or "exploded" across a large, diffuse area. Anna's, broad-tailed, and white-eared hummingbirds are other North American species that sometimes mate in exploded leks. The evidence for species-specific lekking behavior is strongest, however, among calliope and blue-throated hummingbirds of North America.

The males of an exploded lek are close enough to hear one another, and can therefore compete vocally, but are not so close that they compete by seeing and threatening or attacking one another. Males do establish what amount to territories in different sections of a lek and chase other males off these territories. And some males do get territories that because they are nearer to the center of a lek tend to be more desirable. These are sometimes called lek territories. But the territories are not set up around nectar-producing plants, and males in a lek area often interact, with females and other males, mainly by singing and vocalizing. The females tend to arrive at a lek at different times and choose a male. Feeding territories set up by male calliope hummingbirds in British Columbia, beginning at the end of April, became breeding territories after the plants in the territory had stopped producing nectar in early June. The males "commuted" to feed from plants outside their territories but continued to defend their breeding territories for about another month, even though the territories contained no nectar. This is consistent with the exploded lek mating approach that another group of researchers found for male calliope hummingbirds.

Lekking and Coloration

Hermit hummingbirds do not have the bright iridescence that most other species have, and courtship through lekking has sometimes been regarded as a kind of "substitute" for individual flight displays and bright iridescence. It is interesting that male blue-throated hummingbirds are lacking in bright, iridescent coloration and have sometimes been observed engaging in lekking behavior to compete for females. Blue-throated males have some dark blue iridescence on their throats, but their coloration is dull in comparison with the males of most other North American species. In some reports, researchers have categorized the blue-throated hummingbird as a nonlekking species but have identified other species within its genus, *Lampornis*, such as the amethyst-throated hummingbird, as being lekking species. Other researchers have noted that many behaviors of blue-throated males, such as the vicious fights they have with one another, indicate that they do compete and vocalize in leks. It is known, more definitively, that some species in the genera *Lampornis* and *Amazilia* do practice lekking, and some North American species are members of these genera.

Apart from the absence of bright coloration, a similar appearance between males and females has been associated with lekking in some species of hummingbirds. When males and females of a species look very similar, researchers say that the species is sexually monochromatic or monomorphic.

In the case of the white-eared hummingbird, a North American species that researchers have observed lekking, the males and females look more similar than other North American hummingbirds do. The males and females of rufous-tailed hummingbirds also look very similar, and this species, of the genus *Amazilia*, engages in lekking. Although rufous-tailed hummingbirds have vividly green iridescent coloration, the similar appearances of males and females effectively make the males' iridescence less unique. One way of thinking about lekking is as the use of vocalizations and direct competition among males to substitute for the absence of the shock value of male iridescence. But from a scientific standpoint, the evolutionary origins of lekking in relation to coloration are still somewhat mysterious. Only about half of the lekking species of hummingbirds are sexually monomorphic. And calliope, broad-tailed, and Anna's hummingbirds clearly are sexually dichromatic, with the males showing bright patterns of iridescent coloration, and also sometimes engage in behaviors that have been described as lekking.

Nectar Availability

In Anna's, calliope, broad-tailed, and probably white-eared hummingbirds, lekking may have much to do with the availability of nectar in a given area. Even in hermits, lekking is not a fixed, constant behavior that all males practice from year to year. Multiple generations of hummingbirds within a given species, or within a subpopulation of the same species, do not always mate through lekking. Male hummingbirds may lek because they either cannot or choose not to establish feeding territories. Lekking can therefore be seen as going along with traplining. The hermit hummingbirds generally feed by traplining. Researchers think that the nectar-producing plants may be so spread out in a given area, at a given time, as to prevent groups of males from setting up territories. In the North American species that sometimes mate via lekking, the behavior may thus go along with the intermittent need to feed by traplining.

Lek Environments

Scientists have noted other characteristics that sometimes are found to be associated with lekking. Lekking species tend to live in more dense forest environments, and the shortage of bright sunlight may make iridescence, such as in courtship displays, less visible and therefore less practical as a way for males to attract females. Researchers have noted that blue-throated hummingbirds tend to live in areas that are more strongly forested than the areas that other species live in. The bright green iridescence of species in the genus *Amazilia*, such as the rufous-tailed hummingbird, could be viewed as providing camouflage for both males and females in a dense forest and simultaneously nullifying the display value of iridescence for males. But scientists can really only hypothesize about the reasons some nonhermit species of hummingbirds practice lekking. It is possible to say that scientists view lekking as being a "primitive" mating practice, particularly among species of hermit hummingbirds. There are a number of ways in which iridescence in males and females, dive displays for courtship, and even habitat preferences may have interacted and changed during the evolution of different hummingbirds.

Finally, leks at tropical latitudes may be very large and exist in roughly the same locations from year to year. Some leks of the long-tailed hermit hummingbird, for example, are more than 250 yards in length. Across one lekking area in Central America, a hundred or more of these hermit hummingbirds at a time were found to interact, particularly by male-male vocal interactions, with the aim of mating. In this area, some of the leks were used by various hermit hummingbirds for more than twelve years in a row. In the same broader region, scientists located about thirty-two separate leks between July and November of one year.

Flight Displays and Courtship Sounds

Male hummingbirds generally perform U-shaped dive displays, coupled with vocalizations at certain points in the display, to court females for mating. Males sometimes use these dive displays to scare off females or males who are invading their territories. Although this can sometimes mean that a U-shaped dive display has nothing to do with courtship, males of various species tend to use dive displays mainly in front of females and more during the mating months than at other times. The dive displays of some North American species are circular or trace out the shape of an oval. Costa's hummingbirds tend to only make ovular dive displays, and the dive display of the rufous may be either U shaped or oval shaped.

Another flight display that many different species perform is the shuttle display, in which the male flies back and forth in a slightly curved, horizontal path. Males are able to make buzzing sounds with their flight feathers during shuttle displays. Some species, such as the rufous, perform shuttle displays that trace a figure eight. Males of some species, such as the calliope, also carry out hover displays. In a hover display, the male flies up to a point, hovers, and then flies downward, vertically, in a stepwise fashion and continues hovering. The shuttle displays and U-shaped dive displays are the flight displays that are most similar among different North American species.

Using Displays

In general, male hummingbirds use their U-shaped dive display more in front of females than males, either to threaten a female away from its territory or to court her or both. Researchers have noted that territorial males do not very frequently use their U- or J-shaped dive displays to scare off invading males. Male calliope hummingbirds, for example, tended to simply chase males that intruded on their territories and did not perform flight displays. When males use the displays before mating, the males tend to also repeat

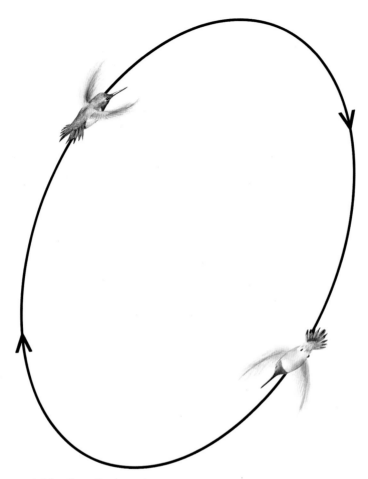

The courtship dive display of the male rufous hummingbird is often oval shaped, although the species will make U-shaped dive displays, too.

them many times. For example, one male hummingbird made nineteen dives, four displays of hovering, and buzzed six times during a shuttle display. In this case, one of the buzzing sounds lasted twenty-six seconds.

Different species of North American hummingbirds do, nonetheless, use different sequences of courtship behaviors and sometimes mate at different sites. In the case of Anna's hummingbirds, for example, the male usually chases the female from its territory and follows it to a site near to its nest. The male then mates with her there. Male calliope hummingbirds, however, do not generally chase females from their territories before mating. For some species, like the calliope hummingbird, this may be one way to tell if a male is treating a female as a potential mate or as just another intruder. At least in calliope hummingbirds, a male that is about to actually mate will probably

The male ruby-throated hummingbird makes a U-shaped dive display as part of its courtship of a female before mating.

thus not both chase and perform a dive display. But a male calliope hummingbird that is still evaluating the female as a potential mate earlier in the courtship process may both chase and perform dive displays. For the casual observer, thus, it is not necessarily possible to conclude that any given male-female interaction is about to involve actual mating or is even part of courtship at all.

Despite the differences in mating behaviors among species, the details of the U-shaped displays tend to be fairly consistent across species lines. The female will typically be perched on a branch, often one that is not very high up, during these U-shaped displays. More specifically, the female usually perches at the center and lowest point of the U and then moves to another nearby perch. Female calliope hummingbirds are known to move from one site to another, while the males follow them and continue performing the displays. Additionally, females of various species may make some attempt, immediately before mating, to display their colored feathers to the male.

A hummingbird may also use variations on its displays to chase other hummingbirds off its territory. Male Anna's hummingbirds, for example, may fly upward and vertically a short distance and make some buzzing noises at an intruder. Next, the male will fly up between 60 and 120 feet and dive downward at a steep angle. A hummingbird will often dive at an invader directly and make a single, threatening sound near the bottom of the dive. Hummingbirds can dive at speeds of up to 65 miles per hour and may dive as many ten times in a row. At the bottom of the dive, however, there tends to be, as one might expect, an upward movement that traces out a U shape.

Courtship versus Chasing

Although the displays used in mating are sometimes indistinguishable from the displays used for chasing intruders, male hummingbirds do perform more displays during the mating season. Researchers have found that male black-chinned hummingbirds perform flight displays when they are wintering in Mexico or other sites. Male Anna's hummingbirds have also been known to perform their dive displays year-round. Researchers have nonetheless found that North American hummingbirds generally use their flight displays, either to chase intruders or to impress females, much more frequently during the breeding months than during the rest of the year. Researchers have found that male calliope hummingbirds actually tend to do more displays for invading males in the first months of breeding but then, toward the end of the season, performed more for females.

Despite the potential for confusion, researchers have noted other ways to distinguish between displays that males perform in either defense or courtship. Female hummingbirds that are ready to mate tend to perch within a male's territory. Scientists have found that males tend to do displays in front of any territorial invader that chooses to perch and that does not simply fly into the territory. Also, the sequences of courtship-associated displays tend to be very prolonged. To court a female, one male calliope repeated the dive display thirty-two times and then performed six hovering displays and seven shuttle displays that included buzzing sounds.

Male hummingbirds also do not generally allow their female mating partners to share access to their feeding territories for prolonged periods of time. Males are known to chase, in an aggressive fashion, their female mates from their feeding grounds. This type of chasing occurs after the actual mating process and therefore cannot be viewed as part of the mating process. Females are thus unlikely to get any prolonged special treatment from their mates.

Mate Cooperation

Males usually do not provide any care for their offspring and sometimes may act aggressively toward nestling hummingbirds. Scientists can more easily monitor the behavior of adult male hummingbirds than female hummingbirds, given that males are more colorful and behave in more demonstrative ways (immature males and females often look similar to adult females). Although males do not seem to specifically exhibit aggression toward their own offspring, males do treat nestling hummingbirds with as much aggression as they treat adults. Female blue-throated hummingbirds, for example, are not always especially protective of their nestlings and will "allow" males to attack nestlings.

The males of some species of hummingbirds do, however, sometimes help their mates with various tasks. Scientists have observed some male fiery-throated hummingbirds, which live at altitudes of a mile or more above sea level in Costa Rica and Panama, allowing one or two females to share some flowers contained within the territories of the males. These temporary episodes of "cooperation" occurred around the times at which the males were mating with the females. Researchers have also observed male hummingbirds sitting on the same branches as their mates were sitting on. A male generally only does this for a few days before or after it has mated. Some researchers have reported that male hummingbirds sit or feed around

It's possible that the gaudy colors sported by male hummingbirds such as the green-breasted mango would attract predators to nestlings if the males helped raise the young.

Body Weight and Flight Displays

Researchers have found that male hummingbirds in particular will sometimes limit or vary their food intakes when they are competing for females or chasing invading birds. During the daytime hours, male broad-tailed hummingbirds that were able to defend territories sometimes ate more frequently than females did and ate less at each feeding than did females. The males only gained between 1 and 2 percent of their body weights throughout the daytime hours.

Researchers think that this strategy of eating small and frequent meals during the day helped the males stay light and thereby fly in an agile manner. At the end of the day, researchers noted that the males ate large amounts of food and often gained, within a relatively short period of time, between 34 and 40 percent of their body weights. Most of this extra weight probably remains in the hummingbirds' crops during these "binges," and the crop gradually allows the nectar to be processed by the birds' digestive tracts. Most hummingbirds do tend to gain weight throughout the day. In hummingbirds that do not limit their food intakes during the day, this weight gain tends to be more gradual and spread out across the day.

the area in which a female with whom it has mated is finalizing a nest or is about to lay eggs. In other cases, a male will chase from its territory, albeit unsuccessfully at times, all females, including its mate or mates. In general, however, it is important to note that hummingbirds tend to be very isolated from other hummingbirds.

Researchers have suggested that the more brilliant colors on male hummingbirds could be detrimental to the viability of their offspring's nest, given that the colors could potentially catch the eyes of predatory birds. The lack of involvement of male hummingbirds in caring for their offspring could therefore be the result of complex evolutionary forces. Researchers have nonetheless noted that brightly colored males of other species of birds do not appear to attract predators to the nests of their offspring. Thus, it is not entirely clear what the reason is for the lack of involvement of male hummingbirds in nesting.

Particularly during nesting periods, females of some hummingbird species are not able to establish clear territories for feeding and will sometimes rely on so-called "prostitution" to get food from males' territories. For example, in purple-throated carib hummingbirds, a fairly large tropical species that lives in the Lesser Antilles islands, females will mate with males,

Interactions of Bees and Hummingbirds

Hummingbirds and bees are generally able to share access to nectar from flowers. *Impatiens biflora* flowers, for example, have long tubes, or nectar spurs, that are filled with nectar. These nectar spurs begin at the bottom of the cup-shaped flower and extend down into the flower. Two species of bees generally obtain nectar from very deep down in the nectar spur; hummingbirds, however, generally only obtain nectar from the uppermost portion of the spur, the very accessible site at which it meets the bottom of the flower. Bees also usually feed on flowers that are covered by other flowers and foliage and are therefore less accessible to hummingbirds.

When hummingbirds are not being very active in obtaining nectar from *Impatiens biflora* flowers, the relative absence of the birds can sometimes cause bees to alter their behavior for obtaining nectar. When hummingbirds were not present in large numbers, it was observed that the bees of two separate species began feeding on more of the flowers in the outermost layers of blossoms, where the hummingbirds had usually fed. In response to the same scarcity of hummingbirds, the bees of another species consumed nectar for longer portions of the day. In short, bees appear to usually stay out of the way of hummingbirds.

and get food from the males' territories two months before the breeding season begins. In January, neither the males nor the females of the species are really physiologically capable of mating successfully. A female typically flies into the male's territory, is chased away about five times, and then returns again. This is similar to the initial courtship process in which North American hummingbirds engage. The male then allows the female to stay in the territory, and the two birds make some vocalizations and aerial displays. The male ultimately mates with the female, sometimes as early as January, even though neither bird is capable of mating successfully until March or April.

CARING FOR THE EGGS AND THE YOUNG

Creating eggs is metabolically taxing to a female hummingbird. Two newly laid hummingbird eggs generally weigh between 10 and 13 percent of the body weight of a female. A female hummingbird is usually ready to lay her eggs one or two days after she has mated. After laying the first egg, hummingbirds do not typically lay the second until one or two days later.

Hummingbirds usually incubate their eggs for between fourteen and eighteen days. As discussed above, female hummingbirds are skilled at maintaining the temperatures of their eggs. Although females sometimes enter torpor for a few hours even when they are nesting, there is evidence that nesting females do not enter torpor as frequently as do females that are not nesting. Females generally maintain the temperatures of their eggs by only leaving the nest for short periods of time and by rotating the eggs at least once a day. This rotation also may prevent the developing embryos from adhering to the insides of the eggshells.

Rapid Growth

Newly hatched hummingbirds grow rapidly and generally remain as nestlings before they fly for only between twenty-one and twenty-nine days. Scientists have observed some hummingbirds losing weight over their first two days of life, but the birds subsequently begin to grow. Within the first twelve to fifteen days of life, rufous hummingbirds are found to grow from 0.02 ounce to 0.12 or 0.13 ounce. This is more than a sevenfold increase in body mass in roughly two weeks. A rufous hummingbird thus reaches essentially its full adult weight before it leaves its nest or begins flying.

Feeding hatchlings is a time- and energy-consuming task that the female hummingbird accomplishes alone. This buff-bellied hummingbird makes numerous regurgitation feedings as the young develop.

Hummingbirds also rapidly exhibit other indicators of physical maturity. Pinlike hints of primary feathers develop by six or seven days after rufous hummingbirds emerge from their eggs. Their eyes first start to open by about nine or ten days after the nestlings have hatched, and their eyes are entirely open twelve or thirteen days after the birds have hatched. At about the same time, the hummingbirds' primary feathers become developed to a degree that allows them to be ready to fly. About two days later, at fourteen or fifteen days after hatching, the birds first start to practice flying. A week or week and a half later, the fledgling hummingbirds begin to fly.

It is also important to note that baby hummingbirds cannot regulate their body temperatures before their feathers have developed. The mother thus has to sit on, to one degree or another, not only the eggs but also the baby hummingbirds for the first fourteen or so days of their lives.

Female hummingbirds typically feed their nestlings by regurgitating food two to three times per hour. The mother has to provide some sort of stimulus, such as tapping the young birds' beaks or making a noise, or the nestlings will not open their mouths in the so-called feeding response. If the nestling does not receive food shortly after having the stimulus applied, the nestling will stop opening its mouth to feed. The mother thus has to reinforce feeding as a learned—as opposed to a purely instinctual—behavior.

Nestling Communication

A nestling hummingbird responds to its mother's feeding sounds and tappings by making sounds and moving its wings in specific ways, not simply by opening its mouth. Females use this tapping to induce the feeding response for about the first five days of the nestlings' lives. After this, but even before the nestlings are able to use their eyes, the nestlings become able to use their incompletely developed wings to feel their mother flying into the vicinity of the nest. The mother essentially displaces the air and produces a little "wind" when it flies in with food, and the nestlings can feel this through the secondary movements of their short feathers. The nestlings open their mouths in response and do not require the tapping anymore.

Hummingbirds generally feed in brief intervals, but this pattern is especially evident in nesting female hummingbirds. Female hummingbirds are remarkably adept at tending to their nests. It is advantageous for hummingbirds to not leave their nests for long periods of time, both to prevent predation and also to maintain the temperatures of their eggs. Hummingbird eggs are extremely small and therefore lose heat very rapidly.

Nesting hummingbirds, according to researchers, leave their nests a number of times each hour but often leave for only a few minutes at a time. Black-chinned and Anna's hummingbirds depart from their nests an average of between 5.7 and 8.6 times each hour during the day. The black-chinned hummingbirds are present at their nests between 66 and 73 percent of the time, despite the fact that the birds are only sitting on their eggs for an average of between 4.6 and 8.6 minutes at a stretch. The Costa's humming-bird leaves its nest for an average duration of between 1.3 and 6.7 minutes at a time. The purple-crowned fairy hummingbird, a tropical hummingbird species in Panama, sometimes leaves its nest for 53 minutes at a stretch but also leaves for periods of only 5 minutes.

Researchers speculate that the relatively constant air temperatures "allow" the tropically nesting hummingbird to leave the nest for longer periods, suggesting that thermoregulation is, in fact, on the mind of the bird. Additionally, hummingbirds that live in tropical latitudes, and at low altitudes—at which the air temperatures are not cold because of high elevations—are known to be capable of breeding and nesting at any point during the year.

Hummingbirds are generally skilled at maintaining their eggs at a rela-tively constant temperature. In a cool climate, an observed Anna's hum-mingbird maintained its eggs at a remarkably constant temperature and was nonetheless away from its nest, in short periods, for a total of one-quarter of the day. In the desert, researchers observed that a Costa's hummingbird sat on its eggs in the morning when the air was still cool and then sat outside the nest, ensuring the eggs were shaded from the direct sunlight, during the hottest period of the day. An Anna's hummingbird was shown, however, to enter torpor for four hours at night, thereby allowing its eggs to decrease in temperature by 68 degrees Fahrenheit.

Mixing Nectar and Insects

Researchers have found that female hummingbirds appear to feed their nestlings insects more than nectar at different stages of development and times during the day. Females give their nestlings mostly insects for the first two days of their lives. Even after the mother has begun to feed its nestlings more nectar, the crops of nestling hummingbirds tend to contain insects more toward the end of the day. This is partly because insects are more active later in the day. Researchers also think that female hummingbirds may have some recognition that nectar provides a burst of metabolic energy in the morning, when the blood sugar levels of both the mother and its nestlings are lowest. Hummingbirds may, on some level, learn that eating protein late in the day will help them stay warm during the night. One of the effects of dietary protein is, in fact, to act as a kind of slow-release form of carbohy-drates, given that amino acids in the fasting state are slowly converted into carbohydrates in the liver.

Young fledgling hummingbirds feed on and share access to the nectar from their mother's flowers for a considerable amount of time. Researchers think that a young hummingbird learns to feed and remember flower loca-tions by first observing its mother's feeding patterns. Later, when humming-birds are migrating for the first time, researchers think that hummingbirds

Hummingbird chicks develop rapidly, often stretching the sides of their nests as they grow. Some two weeks after they hatch, the chicks begin to practice flying.

also learn feeding patterns and techniques from other nonrelated humming-birds. These teachers can be of the same or different species.

Learning
Although hummingbirds are often able to learn things from their mothers for days or weeks, nestling and fledgling hummingbirds are often not nurtured or coddled by their mothers. Researchers observed a female blue-throated hummingbird in Arizona essentially giving up on its first nest in order to start another. The female had begun interacting in courtship behavior with a male hummingbird before its first set of nestlings was fully fledged. After one of its nestlings had died, the mother kicked the remaining nestling out of the nest. This nestling was thought to eventually have died as a result. The researchers suspected that, given that the female had already begun interacting with a mate-to-be, the female had decided to try to concentrate its efforts on the second nest. This is because there was only the potential for it to

successfully raise one nestling, as opposed to the usual two nestlings, from its first nest.

Additionally, nestling hummingbirds appear to learn early on to interact aggressively with adult hummingbirds. Researchers noted that fledgling or late-nestling male blue-throated hummingbirds were often attacked by adult male hummingbirds as soon as they started singing. The young humming-birds nonetheless appeared to be able to "hold their ground" well with adults and learn early in their lives to expect aggressive interactions with other hummingbirds.

Given that hummingbirds reach or even exceed their full adult weights within sixteen days of being born, it is necessary for researchers to use characteristics other than size to distinguish young hummingbirds from adults. One physical characteristic of adult hummingbirds, such as the rufous hummingbird and other species, is a smooth bill. The upper portion of the maxilla, which is part of the bill, of a young hummingbird is corrugated or bumpy. In the wild, however, juvenile hummingbirds are typically very difficult to tell apart from adult females of the same species.

MOLTING, GONADAL CYCLES, AND LIFE SPAN

Most hummingbirds replace their feathers each year, often beginning in the late winter, when the birds are in their winter habitats. The Anna's hummingbird is one exception to this and molts in the summer and fall. The annual replacement of feathers is known to consume a great deal of energy; scientists estimate that between one-fifth and nearly one-half of a bird's normal metabolic rate must be devoted to molting. Consistent with this, the energy output of a molting hummingbird increases by between 5 and 30 percent. This is noteworthy in view of the fact that reproduction in nearly any organism with potentially limited food resources is very costly from the standpoint of the metabolic energy output.

Perhaps not surprisingly, hummingbirds and other birds generally molt at a different time than they mate. Many or most hummingbird species are actually not capable of mating during the annual molt, because the testes then decrease in size. Although this cycle has not been studied in many species other than the Anna's hummingbird, a similar shrinking of the testes, which decreases testosterone levels, probably occurs in most hummingbird species. Researchers have found that male Anna's hummingbirds made many fewer chases and flight displays when their testes had shrunken during their molts. It is also important to note that molting can be a relatively prolonged process, lasting as long as a few months.

Energy Output

Hummingbirds, such as rufous hummingbirds, tend to go into torpor less frequently or for shorter periods of time when they are molting. This makes sense, given that molting requires a large output of metabolic energy.

Although torpor might be expected to conserve metabolic energy and somehow allow more energy to be devoted to molting than to other tasks, this is not really the way torpor works. Torpor essentially puts almost all metabolically demanding growth on hold. Scientists note that molting would take significantly longer if hummingbirds, during molting, spent more time in torpor.

An excessively prolonged molting period may be less than ideal for hummingbirds. Molting requires the blood volume to increase because new blood vessels grow to supply oxygen to the growing feathers. This is somewhat analogous to the increase in the blood volume during human pregnancy, when blood must be shunted to the placenta and developing fetus. In hummingbirds, however, the difference is that the blood flow is increased to the body surfaces where the feathers are growing. This blood flow to the "extremities," potentially increasing heat loss, could invite long periods of dangerous torpor.

Scientists have also noted that an incomplete set of feathers during a prolonged and inefficient molting period may also interfere with aspects of hummingbird flight. Male hummingbirds appear to be less able to put on flight displays during molting. During molting, some male hummingbirds

This photo shows an adult male Anna's hummingbird in the middle of its annual molt. Studies show that molting affects a hummingbird's behavior in a variety of ways.

also lose the normal buzzing sound that they make during shuttle displays. This buzzing sound is produced by the outermost primary feathers, and these are not present at all time points during the molt. Structural differences in the outermost primary feathers of broad-tailed, and to a lesser extent rufous and Allen's, hummingbirds cause these hummingbirds to make a whistling sound when they are flying. These sounds, which are different from the buzzing sound that occurs during shuttle displays, also do not occur at some times during molting. Given that the broad-tailed male seems to rely on this constant sound as a way of essentially broadcasting aggression, it is clear that molting could interfere with the ability of some male hummingbirds to either defend their territories or perform shuttle displays.

Varied Life Spans

Hummingbirds probably live for between two and a half and four years in the wild but may live longer when they are captive. Females tend to live about a year longer than males. A researcher found that one banded female broad-tailed hummingbird lived twelve years in the wild. One blue-throated was found to live six years in the wild, and ruby-throated hummingbirds sometimes live between eight and nine years in the wild. These life spans were all identified through banding experiments. Life spans between nine and twelve years are unusual in the wild but are not that unusual for hummingbirds living in captivity.

5

North American Species

TIPS FOR IDENTIFYING HUMMINGBIRDS

In this chapter, there is a discussion of the characteristics and descriptions of sixteen species of hummingbirds that regularly breed within the United States. There are isolated reports of several other species breeding or passing through this country, but members of these tropical species rarely enter the United States. People have usually only seen these other species in Texas, Arizona, New Mexico, and the Gulf coast states.

There are a number of different factors to consider as you identify hummingbirds. The most simple is your location, given that some hummingbirds have rarely or never been seen nesting in certain locations. There is your location in the broad sense, such as the state you are in, and then there is also the degree of forestation and vegetation and the altitude at which you are observing hummingbirds. Another simple consideration is the time of year. Some species of hummingbirds only or primarily feed and live in the southeastern states, for example, in the fall or winter. Other indicators to look for are the overall size, the presence and brightness of iridescence and other color patterns, the shape of the bill, the presence of orange coloration on the bill, and the flying patterns or muscular movements.

Location and Time of Year

If you take into account both your location and the time of the year, it may be possible to narrow down the possible species of any given hummingbird. For example, the only species of hummingbird that breeds in Alaska and that lives in Alaska at any time of the year is the rufous hummingbird. Similarly, only ruby-throated, rufous, Anna's, calliope, and black-chinned hummingbirds are known to routinely breed in parts of Canada. Moreover, these species are more likely to be present in Canada and the Pacific Northwest between April and August or September than at other times of the year. Anna's hummingbirds live throughout the year in parts of Oregon and even southwestern British Columbia, but the other species that breed in the northern United States are less likely than the Anna's to be present in the fall and winter months.

If you live in Arizona or New Mexico or other southwestern state, there is a much greater diversity of species present. Seven of the species that breed in this country only generally breed in southeastern Arizona, southwestern New Mexico, and sometimes parts of Texas. These are the broad-billed, white-eared, berylline, violet-crowned, blue-throated, magnificent, and lucifer hummingbirds. If you are living in or observing hummingbirds in Arizona, New Mexico, or Texas, it may not be possible to use location alone to identify a given species. If you are at least several hundred miles distant from these areas, however, it is reasonable to assume that you are not going to see one of these seven species.

In the eastern and southeastern states, it is sometimes possible to use the location and season to recognize a member of a given species. Ruby-throated hummingbirds are the predominant species found in the northeastern states. This is particularly true in the late spring and in the summer. The ruby-throated also tends to be the most abundant species in the southeastern states in the summer.

In the fall and winter, members of more species may be migrating through, or even wintering in, the states along the coast of the Gulf of Mexico. One species that winters in significant numbers along the Gulf coast states is the buff-bellied. The distribution of rufous hummingbirds in the fall and winter has, notably, pushed eastward in recent years. Rufous hummingbirds are now quite abundant in the eastern states, especially in the winter along the Gulf coast. They also live in fewer numbers in the fall and winter throughout much of the eastern half of the United States. Black-chinned hummingbirds also are known to winter in the Gulf coast states in significant numbers. Other species that are being seen more and more in these states in the winter months are calliope and broad-billed hummingbirds and, to a lesser extent, Anna's, Allen's, and broad-tailed hummingbirds. These species may be seen in the fall or winter in the northeastern states, farther north than the Gulf coast. In the fall and winter, however, the rufous is more likely than these other species to be present in the Northeast and probably is also more abundant in the Southeast.

Size

One easy way to distinguish one hummingbird from another is by looking at the size or length of the body. Blue-throated and magnificent hummingbirds tend to appear much larger than the other species of North American hummingbirds. Their size can even affect their hovering flight and make them appear to fly more like awkward normal birds and less like elegant hummingbirds. When you are trying to place a hummingbird as a member of any of the other hummingbird species, it is probably not possible to use size alone to identify it. Some researchers view the calliope as the smallest species, on average, but others view the lucifer as the smallest. Although there is variation in the sizes of individual birds within a species, it is possible to say that the Allen's, calliope, ruby-throated, rufous, and lucifer hummingbirds are all quite small.

Shape
Another somewhat salient physical characteristic is the degree of stockiness of a hummingbird's body. Anna's and Costa's hummingbirds have stocky bodies that may appear fat, and this characteristic may help you tell them apart from ruby-throated and rufous hummingbirds. White-eared hummingbirds are also somewhat stocky, and this may set them apart from broad-billeds with similar colorations.

Sounds
Vocal sounds are frequent in many of the species discussed in this chapter, but you will probably not be able to use vocal sounds as a major factor in identifying a species. Some of the species that live throughout the year in Mexico or Central America and only breed in Arizona and New Mexico may make "chip" sounds that are more resonant and have been described as having a metallic character, like the knocking together of small metal objects. Three species whose sounds can have this quality are the broad-billed, violet-crowned, and white-eared hummingbirds. Broad-billed hummingbirds are known for being very noisy and vocalizing almost incessantly while they feed.

Two other species make unusual vocal sounds that may help identify them. Blue-throated hummingbirds, the largest hummingbirds that breed in the United States, are very aggressive and make "snarling," almost growling, sounds when they pursue territorial invaders in flight. The magnificent hummingbird, another large species, sometimes makes a bizarre kind of gargling sound.

Finally, adult male broad-tailed hummingbirds and, to a certain extent, adult male rufous and Allen's hummingbirds have wing feathers that are structurally distinctive and make a whirring or whistling sound when they are flying. Some people have reported being able to hear the sound of broad-tailed hummingbirds' wings across considerable distances.

The Bill or Tail
The color of the bill helps to identify some species of hummingbirds. Beryl-line, buff-bellied, and white-eared hummingbirds generally have orange coloration near the bases of their bills and black on the ends. The bill of the violet-crowned hummingbird is a more rich, dark, reddish orange and is col-

ored across its entire length. Male broad-billed hummingbirds, including juvenile males, also have orange coloration on their bills. The bills of all the other North American species are black.

The degree of curvature of the bill may also help you identify some hummingbirds. Female Costa's and black-chinned hummingbirds have a slight downward curve to their bills. In contrast, the bill of the lucifer hummingbird is more strongly curved downward, which may help you distinguish a lucifer hummingbird from a similarly colored Costa's or black-chinned hummingbird.

The presence of forking in the tail feathers could conceivably be helpful in identifying a hummingbird, but the forking tends to not be especially salient. When the tail is forked, the feathers form a triangle or upside-down V shape. Broad-billed, buff-bellied, black-chinned, ruby-throated, and lucifer hummingbirds all exhibit some forking of their tail feathers. This forking does, however, have the potential to be confused with the normal separation between tail feathers.

Finally, some species make tail movements when they are hovering or flying horizontally. These are the black-chinned, white-eared, and broad-billed hummingbirds. This up-and-down tail motion helps to identify a black-chinned in states outside of Arizona, New Mexico, and Texas. White-eared and broad-billed hummingbirds have similar breeding ranges in those three states, and both make tail movements. The tail movements thus cannot be used to tell them apart. The range of the black-chinned extends up throughout the Pacific Northwest, however. In these northwestern states and in Canada, you may be able to observe the constant tail motion and tell a black-chinned apart from species that look similar.

Coloring in Males and Females

The coloration patterns of a hummingbird's feathers may help you to either rule out certain species or positively identify the species, but the coloration patterns among different species can be remarkably similar. Almost all hummingbirds, both males and females, have some green coloration on their backs. Males tend to have brighter green backs, however, as well as bright, distinctive, iridescent colors on their crowns, which are the fronts of their heads, their throats, and their breasts. Females tend to have mostly gray or white breasts and do not generally have vivid patterns of coloration on their heads or throats. It may thus be possible to detect the sex of a hummingbird merely by the presence of any very bright colors on these parts of the body. In many cases, however, a male or female of one species will look very similar to males or females, respectively, of one or several other species. North American hummingbirds can therefore be surprisingly difficult to tell apart on the basis of coloring alone. Depending on your location, you may be able to narrow down the possibilities. The similarities and differences in coloration among species are discussed in the individual species accounts.

SPECIES ACCOUNTS

This section includes details on the characteristics of sixteen hummingbird species that normally breed in the United States. Some of them are "tropical" species, in the sense that their normal breeding ranges are mostly confined to tropical latitudes in Mexico and Central America. The Tropic of Cancer, an imaginary line at 23.5 degrees north of the equator, runs through central Mexico. All latitudes between this line and the Tropic of Capricorn, the line at the same latitude south of the equator, are tropical latitudes. The main feature distinguishing some North American species from other species that normally breed in the greatest numbers in parts of Mexico and Central America is that they normally breed in the subtropical, temperate latitudes that fall within the United States. They are thus North American and subtropical, temperate breeding species of hummingbirds. But given that some members of these species live all year at tropical latitudes, some species could be considered tropical species.

Each species has a common name and a scientific name. A scientific name is more precise, in the sense that the name minimizes ambiguity in describing a hummingbird. Some hummingbirds have an old common name and a newer common name, and common names can also vary across different languages. The old common name for the magnificent hummingbird, for example, was the Rivoli or Rivoli's hummingbird. Hummingbirds only live in the Americas, and common names for North American hummingbirds would probably mainly be expressed in either Spanish, English, or French. But the use of different common names can still complicate scientific discussions. The common name for the rufous hummingbird is *zumbador rufo* in Spanish. The scientific name, *Selasphorus rufus*, would still be used in Spanish-language journals and would eliminate potential ambiguity.

The sixteen species of hummingbirds in the field guide section fall into ten genera. The following table includes the common names of each of the sixteen species of hummingbirds, as well as a description of some characteristics of the hummingbirds that are members of each genus.

Genus	Common Names	Description
Selasphorus	Allen's, broad-tailed, and rufous hummingbirds	reddish coloration on sides; whistling sound from wings
Calypte	Anna's and Costa's hummingbirds	stocky bodies; males have iridescent "hoods" on the crown and throat
Amazilia	berylline, buff-bellied, and violet-crowned hummingbirds	fairly large; tend to have "bib" pattern of iridescence spanning throat and breast; females and males look very similar; vivid iridescence
Archilochus	black-chinned and ruby-throated hummingbirds	strongly migratory; forked tails; move tails while flying; dark heads with sharply defined violet on throats
Lampornis	blue-throated hummingbird	large; lives in forests at relatively high elevations; white stripes over eyes; not much bright iridescence
Cynanthus	broad-billed hummingbird	small and slim; moves tail when flying; quite vocal
Stellula	calliope hummingbird	the smallest or second smallest hummingbird found in the United States; males have throat feathers that can fan out
Calothorax	lucifer hummingbird	very small; bill curved downward; iridescence on males almost constitutes a "bib"
Eugenes	magnificent hummingbird	large; colorations of males and females strongly differ; males extremely distinctive in appearance
Hylocharis	white-eared hummingbird	white stripes over eyes; orange at the base of the bill

Rufous Hummingbird *(Selasphorus rufus)*

About the name. The genus *Selasphorus* is derived from the Greek and means "light-carrying" or "light-bearing." The species *rufus* comes from the Greek word for red or reddish.

Size. Small

Distribution. The breeding range of this species extends into the north more than the range of any other species and includes the southeastern portion of Alaska, almost all of British Columbia, and parts of Alberta, Washington, Oregon, Idaho, and Montana. The wintering range is concentrated in southern Mexico but includes most of central Mexico and parts of the southeastern United States. Although the breeding populations are most concentrated in the western United States and Canada, rufous hummingbirds are being seen, in quite significant numbers, breeding and migrating and wintering across much of the eastern United States. At least in terms of the numbers of states or area of land in which they may be seen, the rufous has been viewed as the North American species with the largest distribution.

Description. Adult males have orange to reddish brown backs with green spots, but some may have backs that appear mostly green. Adult females have strongly green backs and white throats with brown spots. Males, in contrast, have bright orange or red throats. The bellies and breasts of both males and females tend to be white along the centers and brownish or reddish along the sides. The crowns of both males and females are greenish. Juveniles generally look like adult females.

Look-alike species. Adult female and juvenile rufous hummingbirds are nearly impossible to tell apart from the corresponding Allen's hummingbirds. An adult male Allen's will generally have a much brighter green back and more evenly colored, reddish brown underparts than its rufous counterpart.

Habitat. Their breeding habitat is generally in and around clearings in coniferous forests, such as are found in the Pacific Northwest. When they nest in the summer, as opposed to the spring, they can also live in and around deciduous or mixed forests. During migration, they typically stop in mountain clearings in the Rocky Mountains or the higher elevations of Arizona and New Mexico. In the winter, they live in and around a variety of types of Mexican forests.

Vocalizations. Members of this species make "chip" sounds, isolated "zeek" sounds, and repetitive "zeek" sounds. The dive displays that males perform typically include a series of repetitive "dit" sounds.

Feeding habits. Many males and some females aggressively establish and defend feeding territories. These birds obtain nectar from various flowers that other hummingbirds typically feed from, such as columbines, bee balms, honeysuckles, and red currants. They also rely heavily on insects for food in the spring and eat tree sap from holes that sapsuckers have made.

Distinctive behaviors. Male rufous hummingbirds in particular, and also territorial females, are exceptionally aggressive in establishing and maintaining territories. These hummingbirds migrate the longest distances of any species. They migrate along the Pacific flyway in the spring, between February and May, and along the Central flyway in the late summer and fall. They have slow migrations and are more likely than other hummingbirds to stray from the usual migratory paths, particularly in the fall. Adult males make some whirring sound with their wings, but the sound of the rufous is not as loud as that of the broad-tailed.

Nesting habits. They tend to nest in pine trees in coniferous forests, often in a tree that is near a clearing. The nesting season spans the months of March through July. Particularly later in the nesting season, in the summer months, they may also nest in deciduous trees. Some may nest in the southern portions of the breeding range as early as March.

Broad-tailed Hummingbird *(Selasphorus platycercus)*

About the name. The species name *platycercus* is an amalgamation of two Greek words and simply means "broad tail" or "wide tail."

Size. Medium

Distribution. This species has a large breeding range that spans the Colorado plateau and most other parts of the four corners states and also extends across parts of Wyoming, Idaho, Nevada, and northern Mexico. Some also live year-round in southern Mexico. Those that migrate generally winter in southern Mexico, often near the Gulf or Pacific coasts, but some may winter in the southeastern United States.

Description. The backs of both adult males and females are vivid green, and both also have white breasts and bellies. An adult male, however, has a bright pink or reddish throat and can be distinguished from an adult female on this basis. Adult females have white throats with brown or bronze spots that can appear as stripes. For both adult males and females, the central tail feathers are dark green to brown and the outer tail feathers are dark brown. When viewed from below, the tips of the tail feathers are white. Juvenile males and females look like adult females.

Look-alike species. All broad-tailed hummingbirds look very similar to the corresponding calliope hummingbirds, but calliope hummingbirds have shorter bills. The adult male broad-tailed looks similar to adult male Anna's and ruby-throated hummingbirds. An adult female or juvenile male broad-tailed also may appear very similar to the corresponding rufous or Allen's hummingbirds. One distinguishing feature of the adult male broad-tailed is an almost metallic "trilling" sound during flight. The red throats of calliope hummingbirds also are more streaked and less evenly colored.

Habitat. These birds nest in a variety of forests, including coniferous and deciduous trees, that are in mountainous areas or high elevations. They may also nest and spend time during the breeding months in and around willow or aspen trees. During the breeding season, they live at higher elevations than do most other North American species. They generally live around forests at lower altitudes during the winter months.

Vocalizations. They can make "chip" sounds, but the males appear to not be as vocal as males of other species.

Feeding habits. These hummingbirds eat nectar from many different plants but may have a preference for blue larkspurs, sages, nasturtiums, and penstemons. They eat much tree sap and many insects, including spiders and gnats, when they reach their breeding areas in the spring.

Distinctive behaviors. Some of the males of this species are able to establish territories, but broad-tailed hummingbirds tend to not be as successful at maintaining them as are other North American hummingbirds. The broad-tailed can therefore be viewed as a good example of a facultative trapliner, a hummingbird that traplines when other species are more dominant or when not much nectar is available. They are less aggressive than other species, and rufous hummingbirds are known to be able to displace broad-tailed males from their territories. They migrate along the Central flyway in both spring and fall, but the spring path is farther west than the fall path. Adult males appear to use the unique whirring or whistling sound of their wingbeats in combination with the usual flight displays to make up for their somewhat infrequent use of vocal sounds.

Nesting habits. They nest between April and August. Those that migrate farther north begin nesting later, usually in late May. They make cup-shaped nests, like the nests of other species, and typically build them on a branch that is below another branch and is concealed by the leaves of the pine or deciduous tree. Broad-tailed hummingbirds nest at very high altitudes and can evidently tolerate cold, especially at night, in the mountains.

Calliope Hummingbird *(Stellula calliope)*

About the name. The genus name *Stellula* is derived from the Latin and means "little star" or "little comet" (the streaking pattern of pink on the throats of males does look like a comet). The species name *calliope* is from the Greek and means beautiful. It can also refer to Calliope, one of the nine muses of Greek poetry, who had a beautiful voice.

Size. Small

Distribution. Some of this species breed as far south as southern California and northern Mexico, but the normal breeding range extends from east-central California north through British Columbia. They also breed in western Montana, Idaho, Washington, Oregon, and Nevada. They mostly winter in southern Mexico, but more and more are being seen wintering in the Gulf coast states, especially near the coast.

Description. Both adult males and females have green backs and heads, and both have white breasts and bellies. Adult females have reddish brown coloration along the sides, beneath the wings, but the males are greenish brown along the sides. The throat of the adult male has bright pink streaks, whereas the throats of females are white with brown spots. The tails and bills are quite short. Juvenile males and females look like adult females.

Look-alike species. Juvenile male and female and adult female broad-tailed hummingbirds are bigger than the adult female calliope but nonetheless look similar. Female and juvenile Allen's and rufous hummingbirds also look similar to the adult female calliope but tend to be larger and have more strongly reddish coloration along the sides and under the wings.

Habitat. During the breeding months, they generally live at intermediate to high altitudes, in the coniferous forests of northern California and the Pacific Northwest. During the winter, most of them live at low altitudes and in coniferous or mixed forests.

Vocalizations. When they chase intruders from their territories, calliope hummingbirds can make "chip" sounds. They tend to be less vocal than other species, and males may not even vocalize during their dive displays that precede mating. Males may make a "zing" sound at the lowest points of their U-shaped dive displays.

Feeding habits. This species may be more willing to feed from flowers that are low to the ground. Calliope hummingbirds also eat flies, other insects, and sap from holes that sapsuckers have made. They eat nectar from columbines, honeysuckles, red currants, penstemons, sages, and other plants.

Distinctive behaviors. Calliope hummingbirds tend to orient their tails up and away from their bodies more than other species—at a 90-degree angle—during hovering flight. Males also fan out the feathers on their throat to display their colors to females or appear threatening to territorial intruders. Males may establish breeding territories in exploded leks or assembly areas during part of the breeding season. They tend to use the same migratory pattern as rufous hummingbirds. They migrate north in the spring, along the coast, through the Pacific flyway, and then tend to fly somewhat inland to nest. In the fall, they migrate south along the Central flyway, through New Mexico, Colorado, and western Texas.

Nesting habits. Their cup-shaped nests tend to be exceptionally well hidden, and they often build the nest next to a group of pinecones. This conceals the nest well. Like other hummingbirds, they also camouflage their nests by putting moss or bark on the sides. They also often build new nests on the remnants of old ones. The nest may be high or low in a pine tree. Calliope hummingbirds nest between April and August.

Costa's Hummingbird *(Calypte costae)*

About the name. The genus name *Calypte* is taken from the Greek and means hooded, hidden, or veiled. The coloration of the head and throat of the male Costa's hummingbird does appear as a dark hood. The species name refers to Louis Marie Pantaleon de Costa, a French nobleman and hummingbird naturalist.

Size. Small

Distribution. A large percentage of the Costa's hummingbirds in the United States live here throughout the year, almost exclusively in the southwestern United States. Their year-round range includes the entire Baja peninsula, northwestern Mexico, southern California, and southwestern Arizona. Some of them migrate short distances to breed in Nevada, central California, and more parts of Arizona. Some of them also migrate and winter along the western coast of Mexico, down through central Mexico.

Description. This species appears almost stocky or fat. Adult males have a dark purple "hood" of coloration on the head and neck that can almost appear black. The sides of the adult male's throat are a lighter purple or violet. Adult females have white throats and green or brownish green heads. Both adult males and females have white bellies and breasts and green backs, although the males have brownish green coloration on the sides. Juvenile males look like adult females but may have some dark coloration that is distinctive on their throats, like adult males. Juvenile females look like adult females. The bill is short, black, and may be curved downward slightly.

Look-alike species. Both male and female black-chinned hummingbirds and ruby-throated hummingbirds have similar patterns of coloration but have longer tails and more slender bodies than Costa's hummingbirds. Anna's hummingbirds also look similar, but a male Anna's tends to have brighter coloration on the throat. Adult male lucifer hummingbirds look similar but, unlike the adult male Costa's, have forked tails and longer and more curved bills.

Habitat. Costa's hummingbirds live in the very dry desert environment of the Southwest during the breeding months. They prefer to live near a source of water, such as an intermittent stream. They do not breed in parts of the Southwest that contain real forests. When they are not breeding, some of them live in coniferous or mixed forests at higher elevations.

Vocalizations. They make "tik" and "chip" sounds during dive displays, when they are about to mate or are defending their territories. Male Costa's hummingbirds make a high-pitched, whistling "whee" sound that is sometimes regarded as being an actual song.

Feeding habits. They feed on nectar from penstemons, coral bells, some sage plants, desert honeysuckles, and other plants.

Distinctive behaviors. The dive display that males perform almost exclusively for female intruders or potential mates is unique in being circular and not U shaped. The male starts by flying back and forth a couple of times and then flies in circular loops, sometimes as many as forty times without stopping. The male makes a whistle sound at the lowest point in the circle. Costa's hummingbirds sometimes fly around parts of Oregon, California, and the four corners states during the breeding and nonbreeding months. These flights are not true migrations, and scientists don't know why they make these flights.

Nesting habits. They nest between December and May in southern California and in the Sonoran desert of Arizona. They often build nests in bushes or even cacti, but they also build them in palm trees or deciduous trees. Those that migrate generally reach the southwestern United States between February and April.

Black-chinned Hummingbird *(Archilochus alexandri)*

About the name. The genus name *Archilochus* is an amalgamation of two Greek words and means "chief of a group of military men," indicating that this hummingbird is chief in relation to other species or genera. The genus name was chosen in the nineteenth century and is meant to refer to the Greek poet Archilochus. The species name *alexandri* refers to a medical doctor and naturalist from France, M. M. Alexandre, who discovered the species in Mexico in 1846.

Size. This species is small, and their lengths vary from 2.9 to 3.75 inches. The bill is somewhat long, between 0.6 and 0.9 inch. Females often are heavier and have longer dimensions than males.

Distribution. Only ruby-throated and rufous hummingbirds have more broad distributions than this species. This species breeds throughout northern Mexico, the western and southwestern United States, and the southern portion of British Columbia. Some live year-round in southern Texas or northern Mexico. The wintering range includes the coastal portions of southern Mexico and the United States Gulf coast states.

Description. Both adult males and females have green backs, white bellies and breasts, and greenish gray coloration along the sides. The adult male has a strip of purple coloration along the base of its black throat. The throats of females are grayish or white. Juveniles generally look like adult females, but juvenile males may have black splotches on their throats.

Look-alike species. Ruby-throated hummingbirds look similar but have more vivid colors and shorter bills. Anna's and Costa's hummingbirds look similar but generally have bigger heads and have bodies that are more stocky or round.

Habitat. This species spends the breeding months in and around deciduous or coniferous forests, often at relatively low elevations or in suburban environments. They spend the winter in any number of types of forest environments.

Vocalizations. They make "choo" and "chip" sounds and may make less distinct chattering sounds when they are defending their territories. Males also make a sound at the lowest point of their dive displays that is probably a vocalization.

Feeding habits. This species eats nectar from penstemons, scarlet and trumpet creepers, sages, honeysuckles, and other plants. They also eat insects and sap.

Distinctive behaviors. They tend to move their tails up and down when they hover. Black-chinned hummingbirds are known to band together and mob owls, reptiles, and other avian predators, such as jays. Females may be more territorial than females of other species.

Nesting habits. The outsides of the nests, specifically those built by birds in California, tend to be less thoroughly camouflaged than the nests of other species. Eggs from more than 65 percent of nests are taken by predators, and this high failure rate could be partially a result of the grayish color of the nests. They nest once or twice, sometimes three times, per year and may lay up to three eggs as opposed to the usual two for hummingbirds. They lay their eggs one to two days apart, and the incubation period is between thirteen and sixteen days. The young stay in the nest for twenty-one to twenty-two days. Some may remain fledglings for very long periods of up to fourteen days.

Blue-throated Hummingbird *(Lampornis clemenciae)*

About the name. The genus name *Lampornis* is derived from two Greek words that translate as "radiant bird" or "bright bird." The species name refers to Clémence Lesson, wife of naturalist René Lesson and a French bird enthusiast who observed this species in the early nineteenth century.

Size. This is the largest species that breeds in the United States. Their lengths range from 4.75 to 5.2 inches, and they weigh between 0.24 and 0.33 ounce.

Distribution. Some breed in southeastern Arizona, western Texas, and southern New Mexico. More may now be breeding farther north, in northern New Mexico or Colorado. Larger numbers breed in northern Mexico or live all year in southern and western Mexico, excluding the Baja peninsula.

Description. The backs of both adult males and females are green, especially from the head to the middle of the back. The lower back toward the tail becomes a bronze or gray mixed with green. The adult male has dark cobalt blue coloration on the throat. All blue-throated hummingbirds have gray underparts and dark blue or black tails, and the adult female has a gray throat with some spots. All have bands of white coloration over their eyes, but this does not help distinguish them from species with similar appearances. The wings are dark gray to black.

Look-alike species. Female broad-billed hummingbirds look similar but are smaller. Female magnificent hummingbirds are similar but have more greenish tail feathers.

Habitat. They tend to live at relatively high elevations, often in and around streams that run through canyons. In Mexico, they live in coniferous or deciduous forests and also tend to live around rivers or creeks. This species prefers a wetter environment than do some other hummingbirds.

Vocalizations. They make "seep" and "peep" sounds when they are defending their territories or engaging in courtship behaviors. Adult males make repetitive "peep" or "chip" sounds when they are sitting, and these are sometimes regarded as a song. Both sexes make "snarling" sounds when they are chasing or attacking intruders.

Feeding habits. This species eats some sap and may prefer to feed from plants that have large blossoms, such as mountain and scarlet sages, penstemons, lobelias, and columbines. They also eat a lot of insects during the spring.

Distinctive behaviors. Blue-throated hummingbirds are extraordinarily aggressive and are known to snarl when they are chasing invaders. Males have been observed taking other males of their species to the ground with such force that both birds hit with a thud. They also mob owls and other birds and may fight and hurt hummingbirds they are chasing. Males may engage in lekking when preparing to mate. This species also flies in a manner that is less elegant and more awkward than the flight of other hummingbirds.

Nesting habits. Interestingly, this species prefers to nest in some kind of sheltered structure, such as in a cave, on a cliff, or under some part of a roof or bridge. When they nest in trees, the nests are frequently close to a creek or small river. The nests are cup shaped, and the outsides tend to be concealed with green plant material. In comparison with other species, females are especially likely to use the same nesting location from year to year. Females may even use the same location two to three times in one year. Blue-throated hummingbirds nest in the United States between April and July but may nest as late as September.

Ruby-throated Hummingbird *(Archilochus colubris)*

About the name. The species name *colubris* has been adapted from the word *colibrí*, used by the native Arawak people who lived on Haiti and other Caribbean Islands before the arrival of Columbus. *Colibrí* originally meant something similar to "sky spirit bird" and has a supernatural connotation. In many languages, including French, German, and Italian, the word hummingbird is translated as a variation on the word *kolibri* or *colibri*.

Size. Small. They are between 3 and 3.75 inches in length and weigh between 0.088 and 0.118 ounce. They may weigh as much as 0.176 ounce before they migrate. Females are often noticeably larger than males.

Distribution. This hummingbird has the second-largest breeding range of any North American species. They breed through most of southern Canada, some as far west as western Alberta, and most of the eastern half of the United States. They spend the winter throughout much of Central America and parts of southern Mexico.

Description. Adult males and females have green backs, light gray bellies, and wing feathers that appear black on the sides. Adult males have white breasts and red or magenta throats. Adult females have more evenly gray underparts and throats. The tails of all ruby-throated hummingbirds are forked and form a flattened V shape. Juvenile males and females look like adult females but have bills that are shorter, and juvenile males may be distinguished by the dark spots on their throats.

Look-alike species. Black-chinned hummingbirds look very similar, but a male black-chinned tends to have a more black face and throat and less red coloring than a ruby-throated hummingbird. Female ruby-throated hummingbirds sometimes look like female and juvenile rufous hummingbirds, but a rufous will have more redness than grayness on the tail and sides. Costa's and Anna's hummingbirds have similar colorations but are stockier and generally do not live in the ruby-throated's range.

Habitat. During the breeding months, they live in and around deciduous and coniferous forests and are not very likely to favor more sparsely wooded suburban or urban environments. When they are migrating, they often stop in deciduous forests in the Gulf coast states. They winter in different types of tropical forests.

Vocalizations. This species makes "chew" and "chip" noises, sometimes when perching. They make repetitive "chips" and other sounds when they are chasing intruders.

Feeding habits. Ruby-throateds eat nectar from jewelweeds, columbines, honeysuckles, trumpet creepers, and other plants. This species may rely very heavily on tree sap and insects, particularly during the spring.

Distinctive behaviors. They like to bathe in sprinklers or in other sources of fine water droplets. Many migrate across the Gulf of Mexico, primarily during the northward spring migration, in single flights that take about fourteen to eighteen hours and cover about 500 miles. They tend to use the Central flyway for both spring and fall migrations.

Nesting habits. They nest between April and September, and the nest is usually on a branch that is under another branch. They incubate their eggs between fourteen and sixteen days. Nestlings do not fly until they are fourteen to eighteen, or rarely up to thirty, days old. After they first fledge, they may stay around the nest for up to thirty days. This species typically has two nests and broods per year.

Anna's Hummingbird *(Calypte anna)*

About the name. The species name, *anna*, refers to Anna de Belle Masséna, who was a nineteenth-century Italian duchess. A naturalist saw a member of this species in Anna's husband's bird collection and named it after the wife.

Size. Medium. They are between 3.2 and 4 inches long and weigh between 0.13 and 0.15 ounce.

Distribution. Anna's hummingbirds live throughout most of California, western Oregon, and southern Arizona. Most live in the coastal portions of California and Oregon, but some live as far north as southern British Columbia. Essentially all or most of the Anna's hummingbirds that breed in the United States also live there throughout the year. That said, some of them do move into parts of Nevada or northwestern Mexico during the winter months. These areas should not really be considered a wintering range, given that the seasonal movements of this species are not predictable and are based on altitude and not latitude.

Description. This species, like the Costa's hummingbird, has a stocky body. Adult males have red to magenta coloration on their throats and the fronts of their heads. Adult females have white throats with dark spots. They all have green or blue-green backs and underparts that are gray with white streaks. They all have greenish sides and bills that are medium in length. Juveniles look like adult females, but juvenile males often have some dark gray coloration on their throats.

Look-alike species. Costa's hummingbirds look similar but have smaller bodies and underparts that are more white than the gray of the Anna's hummingbird. Adult male Costa's hummingbirds also have coloration that is more restricted to the sides of their throats than it is in the Anna's. Black-chinned and lucifer hummingbirds may look similar but have more slender bodies.

Habitat. They tend to live at lower elevations, below 6,000 feet, in less densely forested areas. They are comfortable living in urban and suburban environments, in deciduous and dry forest environments. When they are not breeding, they may fly to and live at higher elevations, in coniferous, mountain forests.

Vocalizations. Anna's hummingbirds make "chip" or "chick" sounds when they are chasing invaders. They also make a buzzing or chattering "song" that consists of repetitive "chick" or "zhee" sounds.

Feeding habits. They eat nectar from columbines, fuchsias, sages, penstemons, and other plants. They also eat many insects.

Distinctive behaviors. The males of this species sometimes challenge and scare off invaders in their territories by puffing out their chests while they are perched. They may also move their bodies while still staying perched to make their iridescent throat coloration more obvious. Anna's hummingbirds are also unique in moving relatively short distances at different times of the year to higher elevations.

Nesting habits. They make small cup-shaped nests that are typical of hummingbirds but are willing to use materials found in cities and suburban areas. These include bits of litter or similar materials. The nesting season is prolonged, and birds that live in California tend to nest between December and May. Females incubate their eggs for between fourteen and nineteen days, and juveniles remain in the nest for between eighteen and twenty-three days. The young then begin to fly and may remain near the nest as fledglings for a week or longer.

Allen's Hummingbird *(Selasphorus sasin)*

About the name. The common name, Allen's, refers to and commemorates Charles A. Allen, a birder and taxidermist who lived in California in the nineteenth and twentieth centuries.

Size. Small. They are between 3 and 3.6 inches in length, and they weigh between 0.07 and 0.12 ounce.

Distribution. Allen's hummingbirds breed in a section of land that includes areas along the Pacific coasts of California and the southern tip of Oregon. Some also breed in western Mexico and in Texas or Louisiana. Most spend the winter months in southern Mexico, although some winter along the Gulf coast of Louisiana and Mississippi. When they are migrating, they may stop in parts of Arizona and New Mexico.

Description. Adult males and females have green on their backs, extending much of the way down the back, and on the tops of their heads. Adult males have reddish orange throats and reddish brown coloration around the eyes, on the sides, and on the tails. Females also have reddish brown tails and sides but have dark green or brown spots on their throats. Both males and females have white underparts, but only along the centers of their bodies. Juveniles look similar to adult females.

Look-alike species. Rufous hummingbirds are extremely difficult to tell apart from Allen's, although a rufous tends to have a more spread-out tail than an Allen's. Juvenile and female broad-tailed and calliope hummingbirds also can look similar.

Habitat. They live near the Pacific coast in mixed forest environments at low elevations. This species may have a preference for living around eucalyptus trees in California. They winter in and around mixed forests.

Vocalizations. They make "zeek" and chattering, repetitive "zikkity" sounds.

Feeding habits. Allen's eat nectar from the flowers of eucalyptus shrubs, honeysuckles, columbines, and sages. They freely visit feeders but do not nest as frequently in urban areas as do Anna's.

Distinctive behaviors. This species uses more of a J-shaped than a U-shaped dive display. There is a subspecies of Allen's hummingbirds, *Selasphorus sasin sedentarius*, whose members live throughout the year in the most southern parts of California, on the Channel Islands and coast. They have larger bodies than migratory Allen's and never migrate. The spring migration of Allen's occurs very early in the spring, and they reach their breeding areas between January and March. They may also begin migrating south as early as May, although some do not leave California or Oregon until September. They use the Pacific flyway for both spring and "fall" migrations, but they migrate south along a path that is more inland than their springtime, coastal path. Adult males may make some whistling sound with their wings, but the sound is not as obvious as the sound of the broad-tailed's wings.

Nesting habits. They tend to nest between January and April, although some do nest into July. Allen's hummingbirds build nests in a variety of sites, including bushes and very tall trees. They incubate their eggs between fifteen and seventeen days, and their nestlings fledge after twenty-two to twenty-five days in the nest.

Berylline Hummingbird *(Amazilia beryllina)*

About the name. The genus name, *Amazilia*, refers to Amazili, a female character of the Peruvian Inca people in a novel, *Les Incas*, published in 1777 by the French writer Jean Marmontel. The word Amazili is thought to have simply been taken from the word Amazon. The species name *beryllina* is derived from the Greek word for beryl, transliterated as *berullos*, which refers to a blue-green gemstone.

Size. Medium or large. Beryllines are between 3.5 and 4.25 inches in length and weigh between 0.154 and 0.172 ounce.

Distribution. They breed in southeastern Arizona, southwestern New Mexico, and throughout a large band of western and southern Mexico. Many live throughout the year in Mexico and Central America and breed at those sites. Beryllines are regarded as altitudinal migrants and tend to travel to relatively low altitudes in the winter months. Parts of Mexico could thus be regarded as a "wintering" range for those that breed in the United States, but their movements are not first and foremost latitudinal migrations.

Description. Adult males, and to some extent adult females, have large swatches of coloration on their throats and breasts. The shape of this coloration has been described as a baby's "bib" and spreads down like a napkin tucked under a shirt collar. This coloration is bright emerald green in adult males but is not as clearly shaped in females. Females have whitish throats that are covered with dark, brownish green, scalelike spots. All beryllines have greenish brown backs and reddish brown coloration on parts of their wing feathers and tails. The tops of their bills are black and the bottoms have some orange coloration.

Look-alike species. Buff-bellied hummingbirds look similar to beryllines but have more completely orange bills. Also, the male buff-bellied has purple streaks along the sides under the wings.

Habitat. They live and nest in tropical and subtropical deciduous and coniferous forests, often around streams or bodies of water. They tend to breed in the United States at moderate to high elevations, in canyon and mountain environments. When they are not nesting, they tend to travel to lower elevations but live in similar habitats.

Vocalizations. They make "breer" and "zreer" sounds and also make the repetitive "chip" and chattering sounds that are more common across hummingbird species lines. They also may perch and make a song that consists of repetitive "doot" and "deet" sounds.

Feeding habits. As well as consuming quantities of insects, berylline hummingbirds eat nectar from salvias and many other plants. The males are more able than females to establish feeding territories.

Distinctive behaviors. Beryllines are unique in breeding in the United States in very small numbers. Within Mexico, they are known to be altitudinal migrants and have been found to intermingle, peaking in numbers in February, with wintering broad-tailed, calliope, and rufous hummingbirds in western Mexico. At the same site in Mexico, there has been a second peak in berylline numbers between May and July.

Nesting habits. In the United States, they often nest in Arizona sycamore trees that are in and around canyons. They nest between May and August and would not be expected in this country between October and April. Berylline nests are typical of hummingbird nests.

Broad-billed Hummingbird *(Cynanthus latirostris)*

About the name. The genus name *Cynanthus* has been viewed as an amalgamation of two Greek words, which together mean "flower dog" or "flower hound." The broad-billed can be viewed as "doglike" in the tail movements it makes while hovering. It has been suggested that the *Cynan-* portion of *Cynanthus* was taken, and spelled incorrectly, from the Greek word *kuanos* or *kyanos*, which means "blue." This interpretation is not very clear-cut, although males do have bluish green throats and sides. The name *latirostris* is a joining of two Latin words and means "wide-snouted" or "broad-billed."

Size. They are medium to large in length but not heavy for their lengths. They are between 3.4 and 4 inches in length, have slim bodies, and weigh between 0.105 and 0.131 ounce. Females are slightly smaller than males.

Distribution. They breed in southeastern Arizona, southwestern New Mexico, and northern and central Mexico. Many also live throughout the year in western, southern, and central Mexico. Some have also been seen breeding in parts of California and Nevada and wintering in Texas and Louisiana.

Description. Adult males and females both have dark bluish gray tails and green backs, although the green colors of the male are more vivid. Adult males have bluish green throats and vivid green breasts and bellies. Females have grayish white coloration on the underparts and sides. Juvenile and adult males have bills that are more orange than the largely black bills of females. Juveniles have coloration patterns that are similar to those of adult females.

Look-alike species. A female broad-billed can look similar to a female or even male blue-throated, but the blue-throated will generally be larger. Adult male buff-bellieds have reddish tails and sides but have underparts that can look similar to the adult male broad-billeds.

Habitat. They breed in the United States in areas around canyons and streams that may be fairly dry and sparsely forested. When they live or winter in Mexico, they live in deciduous and mixed tropical forests.

Vocalizations. Broad-billed hummingbirds are known for being very vocal when they are hovering and flying horizontally. They make a very jarring, almost metallic chattering sound that is made up of "chit" and "jit" sounds and may be mistaken for the sounds of some insects.

Feeding habits. They eat some insects and eat nectar from honeysuckles, tree tobaccos, and agaves.

Distinctive behaviors. Although broad-billeds are regarded as being less aggressive than many other North American species, their incessant vocalizations have an assertive component to them. Some naturalists have suggested that they use their sounds to establish territorial dominance over other hummingbird species. They also move their tails up and down all the time they are flying.

Nesting habits. This species tends to build nests that are well hidden and likely to be near the ground in a tree or bush. They reach the United States and begin nesting in March or April; some may nest as late as September. Broad-billeds commonly nest two times per season. Their movements within Mexico appear to be mostly seasonal and latitudinal, and researchers do not classify the broad-billed as an altitudinal migrant.

Buff-bellied Hummingbird *(Amazilia yucatanensis)*

About the name. The species name, *yucatanensis*, is taken from the Latin and means "of the Yucatan."

Size. Large. They are between 3.6 and 4.25 inches in length, and they weigh between 0.13 and 0.143 ounce. Males are slightly larger than females.

Distribution. This species lives throughout the year and breeds in the spring and summer along the Gulf coast of southern Texas and Mexico and throughout the Yucatán peninsula. Some actually winter farther north, along the Gulf coast, in Louisiana, Mississippi, Alabama, and Florida.

Description. Like beryllines, buff-bellied males and females have "bibs" of green coloration that cover their throats and breasts. The males and females of this species look remarkably similar and both have green backs, reddish brown tails, and spots of purple coloration along the sides and on the back. The bellies of males are more reddish brown in comparison with the females' grayish brown color, and males have flattened V-shaped tails. The bills of both sexes are mostly orange and have black on the ends.

Look-alike species. Beryllines, particularly males, look similar to buff-bellied hummingbirds but have darker, more purplish tails. The range of the berylline in the United States is unlikely to overlap with that of the buff-bellied, except perhaps in parts of southern Texas.

Habitat. Buff-bellied hummingbirds live and breed mainly in wet, tropical or subtropical deciduous forests. They do not appear to require particularly dense forest environments to live, and they can live in suburban areas and visit feeders.

Vocalizations. They are loud. They make "chip" or "chik" sounds when they are feeding or defending their territories. They also make repetitive "see" sounds when they are confronting territorial invaders.

Feeding habits. This species eats tree sap and insects and nectar from sages, coral bean shrubs, various hibiscus species, and other plants.

Distinctive behaviors. They are quite aggressive and use their fairly large size and loud vocalizations to establish and maintain their territories, often at the expense of other species of hummingbirds. Some of this species migrate "north" or eastward in the fall, and winter along the Gulf coast states. This is unusual.

Nesting habits. The buff-bellied hummingbird tends to build nests within several feet of the ground, in bushes or trees. In the United States, the only buff-bellied nests are likely to be seen in Texas, between March and August or September.

Magnificent Hummingbird *(Eugenes fulgens)*

About the name. The genus name *Eugenes* is taken from the Greek and translates as "well born" or "well bred" or even "noble." The name *fulgens* is derived from the Latin and means "shining" or "glittering." This species was first known by the common name "Rivoli's hummingbird," referring to the Italian duke of Rivoli, François Victor Masséna. He collected bird specimens and provided financial support to scientists or naturalists in the 1800s. The Anna's hummingbird was named after his wife.

Size. They are large but are slightly smaller than blue-throated hummingbirds. They are between 4.5 and 5.35 inches in length and weigh between 0.226 and 0.352 ounce. Males are larger than females.

Distribution. They breed in parts of Texas, southeastern Arizona, southern and central New Mexico, and also northern Mexico. Many live throughout the year across much of Mexico and parts of Central America. Their breeding range includes fairly large parts of Arizona and New Mexico, in comparison with other species that have similar distribution patterns. Some have been seen nesting in Colorado, Nevada, and Utah. Those that breed in the United States generally winter in Mexico or Central America.

Description. All magnificents have green backs. Adult males are very distinctive and have bellies and breasts that are black but have greenish iridescence that is visible from some angles. Males have dark brown tails with bronze highlights, purple coloration on the fronts of their heads, and bright turquoise throats. Adult females have white or gray underparts, green on the sides, and dark brown tails that have greenish highlights.

Look-alike species. Female blue-throateds and magnificents look very similar. Female magnificents are larger than female black-chinned hummingbirds but have similar coloration patterns.

Habitat. They live and breed in deciduous, coniferous, and mixed forest environments, often near a stream or river. They tend to live at somewhat high altitudes, between 4,900 and 9,000 feet.

Vocalizations. They make "chip" sounds when they are feeding and repetitive chattering sounds when they are chasing a bird that is competing for nectar. Magnificents make guttural sounds, which have been described as gargling or "gurgling," when they are challenging other hummingbirds or in other situations.

Feeding habits. Magnificents appear to eat very large numbers of insects and, more than other North American species, may eat more insects than nectar. They do eat some nectar from columbines, sages, penstemons, and other plants.

Distinctive behaviors. Their most unusual behavior, among North American species, is their heavy use of traplining to feed. Traplining magnificents may challenge other hummingbirds, but the feeding area may change from day to day and is not fixed. Traplining is generally only used by tropical species of hummingbirds. Some magnificents do, however, set up feeding territories. They also appear to be prone to massing or banding together in groups of up to a hundred birds that can almost be regarded as flocks. Magnificents have used this behavior to defend nectar sources, making the behavior dissimilar from the mobbing of predators.

Nesting habits. This species usually builds nests fairly far off the ground on a flat branch of a tree. They nest in the United States between April and July or August.

Lucifer Hummingbird *(Calothorax lucifer)*

About the name. The genus name *Calothorax* is an amalgamation of the Greek words *kallos*, which means beauty, and *thorax*, which means chest. Thus, *Calothorax* translates as "beautiful breast" or "beautiful chest." The species name is derived from two Latin words, *lucis* and *ferro*, and translates as "light-bearer" or "torch-bringing." The species name is sometimes described as being of Greek origin, but the equivalent Greek word would actually be *eosphoros*.

Size. They are quite small in weight but medium in overall length. Their bills are very long in relation to their bodies. Thus, a good portion of their 3.2 to 4 inches of length consists of their bills. They weigh 0.097 to 0.134 ounce.

Distribution. They breed in southeastern Arizona, southwestern New Mexico, southwestern Texas, and southern and central Mexico. The area in and around Big Bend National Park, in Texas, is known to be a major site for the breeding of lucifers. They have more of a true wintering range, in southern Mexico, than other species that only breed in the extreme southwestern United States. Many also live the entire year in southern and central Mexico.

Description. The very long bill, which is noticeably curved downward and is black, is an important distinguishing feature of this species. Males have purple throats, white bellies, and black tails. Both males and females have light brownish green backs and sides. Females have white throats and underparts. Lucifers also have tails that appear elongated, very slim, and forked when they are perching. Juveniles generally look like adult females.

Look-alike species. Female and juvenile black-chinned and Costa's hummingbirds have similar coloration patterns and may have slight curvature to their bills. The curvature of the bills of these species is generally very subtle, however, unlike that of the lucifer. Male black-chinned and broad-tailed hummingbirds also can look similar, but the lack of curvature in the bills of these males can help set them apart from male lucifers. Male and female broad-taileds, in particular, have bills that are completely straight.

Habitat. Lucifers breed and nest in the United States in fairly dry areas that are often somewhat harsh and sparsely forested. The species gravitates toward desert environments. They tend to live, both in Mexico and the United States, in and around the deciduous "forests" that are in desert canyons and that may be near intermittent streams. They live at a range of elevations, between 3,800 and 7,500 feet.

Vocalizations. They mainly make "chip" sounds when they are defending their territories or nests or during courtship behaviors.

Feeding habits. Lucifers tend to eat a lot of their nectar from agaves and actually prefer it over other plants. They also get nectar from honeysuckles, penstemons, and other plants.

Distinctive behaviors. They may set up territories that are smaller than those of other hummingbirds, and they do appear to eat from and nest in agaves. Both males and females are fairly territorial and are evidently able to use their small bodies to defend against and fly around territorial challengers. Lucifers have larger distinct wintering ranges within Mexico than other species.

Nesting habits. This species tends to nest low to the ground in an agave, cactus, or other tree or bush. They tend to breed and nest between April and August or September in the United States. As with other species, they often build two or even three nests during a breeding season.

Violet-crowned Hummingbird *(Amazilia violiceps)*

About the name. The species name *violiceps* is primarily viewed as being of Latin origin and translates as "violet head." The *"–ceps"* portion of the name is also sometimes regarded as having originated from the Greek word for "head."

Size. Large. This species is third in average size among North American species. They are between 3.8 and 4.5 inches in length and weigh between 0.183 and 0.208 ounce.

Distribution. They breed in the United States in southeastern Arizona and southwestern New Mexico, but the population within the United States is probably very small. Guadalupe canyon, in southern Arizona and New Mexico, is one site at which some of this species are likely to breed. Larger numbers breed in northwestern Mexico. Many live throughout the year in western Mexico, excluding the Baja peninsula, and tend to live within a couple hundred miles of the coast.

Description. Male and female violet-crowned hummingbirds are almost indistinguishable and have bright white throats and underparts and bluish violet coloration on their heads. The greenish brown coloration on their backs and tails is not very bright. Adults have dark orange bills, which may appear red, with black on the end. In the case of juveniles, about one-third of the end of the bill can be black. This may help distinguish them from adults.

Look-alike species. There are no species that look similar and are generally found within the United States.

Habitat. This species tends to live and breed in fairly heavily forested areas, usually near streams or rivers. These forested areas tend to have a lot of Arizona sycamore trees, in particular. The species tends to not live in open desert environments.

Vocalizations. When they are confronting territorial challengers or invaders, they make jarring, almost metallic-sounding, repetitive "tick" sounds. Males, in particular, also make various sounds when they are sitting, and these sounds have sometimes been regarded as a "song."

Feeding habits. They feed on insects and eat nectar from penstemons, agaves, honeysuckles, and other plants. A few of this species have been seen spending the winter around feeders in the United States, such as at the Banning Creek Field Station in Arizona.

Distinctive behaviors. This species is regarded as being fairly aggressive, but information on their territorial habits and feeding strategies is lacking. The violet-crowned hummingbird has been observed making dives into bodies of water, almost like belly flops, and this is apparently a method of bathing.

Nesting habits. This species is known to build its nests fairly far from the ground, often in sycamore trees. In the United States, the violet-crowned hummingbird nests between June and September.

White-eared Hummingbird *(Hylocharis leucotis)*

About the name. The genus name *Hylocharis* was taken from two Greek words and means "forest grace" or "woodland beauty." The species name *leucotis* is an amalgamation of two Greek words and translates as "white-eared," even though it is not actually the ear of this species that is white. Rather, the species has a white stripe over and behind its eye.

Size. This species is medium in size and is between 3.3 and 4 inches in length. It weighs between 0.113 and 0.137 ounce. Females may be very slightly smaller than males.

Distribution. White-eareds breed in southwestern New Mexico, southeastern Arizona, and in some parts of western Texas, such as in the vicinity of Big Bend National Park. They also breed and live throughout the year throughout much of Mexico and parts of Central America.

Description. Adult males have black heads, with some dark blue color on the crowns, white stripes over their eyes, and green coloration on their throats and sides. Both males and females have brownish green backs and white along the centers of their bellies, with green on the sides. Adult females and juveniles also have white stripes over their eyes but have white throats and more white on their underparts than do adult males. All white-eareds have bills that are about half orange, with the orange extending from the base of the bill.

Look-alike species. Female and juvenile broad-billed and white-eared hummingbirds can look similar, but white-eareds tend to be stockier and to have more green coloration on the sides.

Habitat. They breed in coniferous forests in the United States, generally at fairly high elevations. In Mexico and Central America, they also tend to live in tropical forests at higher elevations, between 3,000 and about 10,000 feet.

Vocalizations. They make "chip" and "chick" sounds, and their sounds may have the kind of clinking quality, as of metal on metal, that seems to occur in some tropical hummingbirds.

Feeding habits. They eat nectar from a variety of plants. Even though most live throughout the year in tropical environments, they are not specialized for one type of flower.

Distinctive behaviors. The white-eared is aggressive and often dominant over other species when multiple species are in a given area. In this context, they are able to change directions efficiently and use their relatively small bodies to their advantage. Like the broad-billed, this species moves its tail when it is hovering. Thus, this behavior cannot be used to distinguish between the two species. The species does move seasonally within Mexico. In one site in western Mexico, there was a dramatic increase in the numbers of white-eareds between April and July. There was a much smaller peak around February, and the seasonal variation for this species was much more pronounced than for other resident tropical species. Scientists have sometimes observed this species lekking.

Nesting habits. They breed and nest in the United States between April and August and may nest twice per year. White-eareds tend to build their nests fairly near to the ground, such as on a bush or low tree branch.

6

Watching Hummingbirds

Large numbers of people enjoy watching hummingbirds at feeders, but some people are also finding ways to observe hummingbirds in the wild. In parts of southern New Mexico, it is possible to see and hear hummingbirds in casual settings. Although the density of nectar-producing plants may not be as great or as consistent in a small city as in some sites outside of cities, you may not have to venture far from civilization to see hummingbirds living in the wild.

WHEN TO GO

Especially if you live outside of the southwestern United States, you are most likely to be able to observe hummingbirds between April or May and September. Even in the Southwest, the numbers of breeding hummingbirds will be greatest during the months between April and October. The major species that migrates north through the eastern half of the United States is the ruby-throated hummingbird. This species arrives in the Gulf coast in early March, the central United States in April, and the northern states of the eastern and midwestern United States by May. The same general pattern holds for the spring migrations of black-chinned, broad-tailed, and rufous hummingbirds in the western states. Calliopes also tend to reach southern Canada and the northernmost states of the Pacific Northwest by May or June. Rufous hummingbirds tend to arrive in the Pacific Northwest earlier, however, in March and April. You may thus want to wait until June in a northern state, when the full populations have arrived, to have the best chance of watching hummingbirds.

Specific locations in the southwestern United States can be considered prime locations for viewing hummingbirds in the wild, and the different species at these locations are most numerous during certain months. There is a possibility of seeing any of at least ten of these hummingbird species in Ramsey Canyon or Madera Canyon in Arizona during the months between April and October: Allen's, Anna's, berylline, black-chinned, blue-throated, broad-billed, lucifer, magnificent, violet-crowned, and white-eared hummingbirds. Most of these ten species also nest in the summer at various other sites in Arizona, and also in Texas or New Mexico. Migratory hummingbirds may also pass through southern Arizona or New Mexico, generally in August or September. Broad-tailed, black-chinned, and calliope hummingbirds are three species that can pass through southeastern Arizona and southwestern New Mexico in August or September.

In the fall, winter, and early spring, California and the Gulf coast states are probably the areas in which you are most likely to see hummingbirds. Several species are wintering along the Gulf coast in Texas, Louisiana, Mississippi, and even Florida. Moreover, ruby-throated hummingbirds, in the spring and fall, and rufous hummingbirds, probably especially in the fall, can pass through these areas on their migrations or decide to winter along the Gulf coast. Many Anna's hummingbirds spend the winter in California, and some species, such as the rufous hummingbird, begin migrating north through California in the late winter.

Hummingbirds are likely to be active throughout most of the day. Although some territorial hummingbirds may eat more nectar late in the day, this is usually the result of their having to fly around all day in defense of their territories.

WHERE TO GO

When you are looking for hummingbirds, it is helpful to keep in mind a number of things about their habitats. Given the opportunity, many species tend to nest and live around a stream or small river. In dry or desert climates, much of the vegetation is around rivers. But hummingbirds may also drink from or clean themselves in bodies of water. Some species, such as the broadtailed and calliope hummingbirds, often nest at high altitudes, above 10,000 feet. Numerous other species tend to nest at various altitudes between about 3,000 and 8,000 feet.

At any altitude, however, it is also reasonable to look for coniferous and deciduous trees that are near to clearings. Although hummingbirds often nest in trees, the nectar-producing plants are likely to be more abundant in the extra sunlight provided by forest clearings. That said, hummingbirds do appear to be more likely to visit flower patches or gardens that are near to trees and not completely out in the open. Trees provide hummingbirds with covered areas in which to build nests and also interfere with the abilities of predatory birds to see a hummingbird feeding. Many territorial hummingbirds also like to have some places, usually on trees, to perch high above the plants in their territories. These perches help them defend against intruders.

Diverse hummingbird species breed at specific locations in the Southwest. The land in and around Ramsey Canyon, which constitutes the Ramsey Canyon Preserve, is owned and operated by the Nature Conservancy.

Prime Sites for Watching Hummingbirds in the Summer

Arizona–Sonora Desert Museum, near Tucson, Arizona

Banning Creek Field Station, Arizona

Big Bend National Park, southern Texas

Guadalupe Canyon, southeastern Arizona and southwestern New Mexico

Madera Canyon, about 45 miles from Tucson

Patagonia–Sonoita Creek Preserve, about 60 miles from Tucson

Ramsey Canyon Preserve, about 90 miles from Tucson

This preserve is southeast of Tucson and is roughly 90 miles from the city. The Nature Conservancy runs organized nature walks through the preserve. Madera Canyon is located about 45 miles south of Tucson. Other sites in the Southwest include Cave Creek Canyon and Green Valley, in Arizona, and Guadalupe Canyon, which stretches between southeastern Arizona and southwestern New Mexico. Several of the species that only breed in Arizona and New Mexico may nest at any number of locations, particularly in central and southern Arizona, between April and September. The land in and around Big Bend National Park, in Texas, is an area where lucifer, white-eared, and blue-throated hummingbirds may be seen between April or May and August. Southern New Mexico, even as far east as Las Cruces, is also generally an area in which there is a great diversity of hummingbird species in the summer months.

Some other locations may especially appeal to hummingbird watchers. The Patagonia–Sonoita Creek Preserve, one site in southeastern Arizona that is popular among birders, is known to be a nesting site for various species of hummingbirds. The Nature Conservancy runs and owns the land on this preserve, which is about 60 miles southeast of Tucson. Another place that sometimes attracts some of the more rare hummingbird species that are found in the United States, such as the violet-crowned, is the Banning Creek Field Station in Arizona. Some of these species even winter here. If your goal is to see some of the species that do not breed in the United States in large numbers, visiting this type of feeding station may allow you to see these hummingbirds. Finally, the Arizona–Sonora Desert Museum, near Tucson, keeps seven species of hummingbirds in an aviary. It is also possible to see hummingbirds outdoors near the museum.

PHOTOGRAPHING HUMMINGBIRDS

Although it is more difficult to photograph hummingbirds in the wild than at a feeder, you can use some of the same approaches. In either case, it is generally advisable to set up a tripod or stand in one location. If you are photographing hummingbirds at a feeder, set up the camera at least several feet from the feeder. Find a feeder with only one feeding site to allow you to focus and direct the camera there. If you are away from a feeder, find a nest or locate a flowering plant that you have seen hummingbirds feeding from regularly. Photographers also recommend that you usually use a flash for photographing hummingbirds, especially in the shade but, ideally, even in bright sunlight. A number of variables that come into play when photographing hummingbirds will be briefly discussed below.

Distance

To ideally focus from a distance, hummingbird photographers generally recommend using a digital camera with a 5X to 12X optical zoom feature in order to magnify the feeder or other site by five to twelve times. A digital zoom feature does not work as well as an optical zoom. It is not clear if the small built-in optical zooms on digital cameras work as well as the larger zoom lenses that are built into higher-end digital cameras. In any case, the optical zoom will let you take the photographs from a certain number of feet away from the hummingbird.

Photographers generally recommend that you photograph a hummingbird with the camera at roughly the same distance above the ground as is the hummingbird. This may complicate the hanging of a feeder. You could hang the feeder near a window, but putting a feeder on or near a window may cause hummingbirds to fly into the window and die. It may instead be possible, by hanging the feeder 6 to 8 feet from the ground, to then position a chair on a hill or other nearby site level with the feeder. Another strategy, putting a piece of white cardboard behind the feeder, allows the body of the hummingbird to contrast with the white background that the cardboard provides.

Shutter Speed and Flash Duration

Getting a sharp image of the wings when photographing hummingbirds has to do with the relationship between the shutter speed and the flash duration. Any shutter speed faster than $\frac{1}{500}$ of a second will essentially "freeze" the movement of a hovering hummingbird's body because the body is never moving very rapidly. Photographers often use faster shutter speeds, however, in the range of $\frac{1}{1,000}$ to $\frac{1}{1,600}$ of a second. The main challenge, therefore, is capturing a still image of a hummingbird's wings. The only way to truly freeze an image of the wings is to take the photograph when the wing is at the peak of the upstroke or the downstroke. The wing slows down and stops for a split second at these points and then reverses directions. At all other points in the wing stroke or wingbeat, the wing is moving too rapidly for

Photographers in the tropics who have a good camera and lots of patience might be able to capture stunning images like this male blue-crowned woodnymph.

most shutter speeds to completely freeze it. There will always be more blur at these points. Being serious about getting a still image of the wings requires taking at least several pictures and happening to take one at the split second that the wing tips are reversing direction. Many photographers, however, actually prefer seeing some blur in the wings. One strategy would thus be to not bother with the flash issues discussed below and use a fast shutter speed, between $\frac{1}{1,000}$ and $\frac{1}{2,000}$ of a second or faster, in the sunlight. As discussed below, using a fast shutter speed with a high-speed sync feature on the flash is another approach.

Photographers sometimes say that the flash duration is the most important variable to consider in photographing hummingbirds with a flash, but it is really also the relationship between the shutter speed and the flash duration. If you really want to freeze as much of the hummingbird's wing movement as possible and illuminate it, you will probably benefit from having a digital camera with a sync speed of $\frac{1}{250}$ or $\frac{1}{500}$ of a second or faster. The sync speed is the maximum shutter speed at which the flash "works."

The overall idea is that "stop-action" photography, such as of a hummingbird's wings, requires the flash duration to be very brief and requires the flash to be synchronized properly with the opening and closing of the shutter. This is because the shutter speed is almost always longer than the flash duration for this type of photography. To photograph hummingbirds, for example, photographers generally have to use a flash duration that is between $\frac{1}{3,000}$ and $\frac{1}{5,000}$, or even as high as $\frac{1}{30,000}$, of a second and a shutter speed that is between $\frac{1}{500}$ and $\frac{1}{1,600}$ of a second or shorter. The problem is that normal flashes cannot be used at shutter speeds faster than the maximum sync speed, which tends to be $\frac{1}{500}$ of a second.

A flash that pulses repetitively, part of the so-called "high-speed sync" feature of some digital cameras, can sometimes help prevent the problem with the flash synchronization by creating many flashes in a row. High-speed sync allows you to use the flash at very fast shutter speeds. Some photographers find that using high-speed sync with a fast shutter speed, between $\frac{1}{1,000}$ and $\frac{1}{1,600}$ of a second, is useful for photographing hummingbirds. Ideally, however, photographers generally recommend getting a digital camera with a high true sync speed. Some higher-end digital cameras use electronic shutters, instead of mechanical shutters, and can have extremely fast shutter speeds, between $\frac{1}{8,000}$ and $\frac{1}{16,000}$ of a second, and also higher true sync speeds. The most serious photographers say that high-speed sync is not a true substitute for a high true sync speed used with one or more normal flashes set at short flash durations.

Since the intensity of the flash of light decreases as you decrease the flash duration, serious photographers sometimes mount three flashes on a digital camera. This can allow you to get more intensity and still use a short flash duration. You can adjust the flash duration on many digital cameras, and the power or intensity of the flash decreases as you decrease the flash duration. If you do not want to mount more flash units on a camera, you may be able to compromise with a flash duration that is longer than $\frac{1}{30,000}$ of a second and shorter than $\frac{1}{3,000}$. This will probably require you to be closer to the hummingbird and will make the flash more intense than it would be at $\frac{1}{30,000}$ of a second.

The f-stop setting is another variable that can be important. The f-stop setting determines the size of the aperture produced by the opening of the shutter, so that higher f-stop settings make the aperture smaller. For hummingbird photography in the sun, photographers generally use a high f-stop setting (f/11 or f/16 or even f/22) with a fast shutter speed. Since some digital cameras do not allow you to use a high f-stop setting with a fast shutter speed, it is worth considering which f-stop settings you can use at a fast shutter speed.

Higher ISO settings can allow you to take pictures in darker conditions but can make a picture grainy. Photographers sometimes use ISO settings of 200 to 400 for photographing hummingbirds, but lower ISO settings, such as 100, will tend to sharpen images in photographs and are probably most desirable. You generally need bright light to use a low ISO setting.

In summary, photographing still images of hummingbirds ideally requires a camera that has either a high true sync speed or a high-speed sync feature coupled with a fast shutter speed, or both. It is also desirable to have a camera that lets you use a fast shutter speed with a range of f-stop values.

7

Hummingbird Feeders

FEEDER SETUP

Setting up hummingbird feeders is perhaps the easiest way to observe hummingbirds. It should be possible to attract hummingbirds to a feeder in any state in the United States, excluding Hawaii and including parts of southern Alaska, and in many parts of southern Canada. Various shapes and types of feeders are available, but you may want to think about some things before choosing and placing a feeder. If you plan on photographing hummingbirds at your feeder, you may want to place it at a site that allows you to sit and photograph the feeder at eye level. It is also worth considering some ways to ensure the safety of hummingbirds visiting the feeder and avoid attracting insects to it.

FEEDER MAINTENANCE

Hanging up a hummingbird feeder might seem like a simple task, but doing basic maintenance is necessary for the health of the hummingbirds feeding from it. This maintenance usually involves cleaning the feeder at least once a week, but every three or four days is better. If the weather is 60 degrees Fahrenheit or higher, many experts recommend cleaning the feeder every two days. The presence of the sugar in the solution, and the water itself, can provide perfect conditions for the growth of bacteria, fungi, and molds. A hummingbird that eats or is otherwise exposed to these bacteria and fungi can die from an infection. Cleaning the feeder and replacing the artificial nectar at the same time is very important.

To clean the feeder, it is advisable to scrub it with a solution of one part bleach, by volume, to ten parts of water. To clean the small openings in the feeder, try pipe cleaners.

Although the task of cleaning a feeder so frequently may seem burdensome, a safe and healthy feeder can provide hummingbirds with a very valuable and important source of food. The same hummingbirds may return

Hummingbirds, such as this female lucifer, can obtain a significant amount of much-needed energy from a well-maintained backyard feeder.

to a feeder year after year. The nourishment that a feeder provides to a hummingbird, moreover, can be very substantial. Researchers have found that a single long feeding may provide a hummingbird with up to 10 percent of its nectar supply for the day. This might only occur if the hummingbird feeds for a long interval of time—a minute or so. But it is helpful to remember that hummingbirds may rely heavily on a feeder. Providing hummingbirds with a healthy, high-quality source of food can have a positive impact on their health.

No Honey or Oils

Never use honey as a source of nectar. Honey is a good medium for growing fungi that can cause hummingbird infections. One type of infection causes a swelling of the hummingbird tongue and can kill the birds. The use of petroleum jelly or other oils on hummingbird feeders is also potentially problematic, although less so than the use of honey. Some people have suggested that putting petroleum jelly or edible commercial oils, such as canola oil or the like, on different parts of feeders can prevent bees and other insects from "perching" and eating the artificial nectar. A buildup of these oils, however, can harm hummingbirds. A final thing to stay away from is the red colorings that are sometimes recommended to color the artificial nectar. These compounds have to be metabolized or excreted and have the potential to harm hummingbirds.

You can use other strategies to prevent insects from honing in on your feeder. Putting up a butterfly feeder can divert butterflies to a part of your yard that is separate from the hummingbird feeder. You can order a butterfly feeder from catalogs that sell supplies for bird enthusiasts. To keep ants off your feeder, bird enthusiasts have recommended putting up some sort of water barrier. Given that ants cannot or will not swim or float across water, some people set up feeders on poles that essentially "rise" up out of the center of a bucket of water, near the ground. You will probably be able to find a hummingbird feeder with a built-in ant guard. Similarly, most hummingbird feeders have fanned-out plastic around the feeding holes that serves as a bee guard.

Another strategy to prevent bees from feeding is to get a hummingbird feeder that you can fill only part of the way so the surface of the artificial nectar solution is lower than the feeding holes. This prevents bees from accessing the nectar but still allows hummingbirds, with their long bills and tongues, to reach down through the holes and feed. If you do use this approach, you may have to get a feeder that has a flattened shape. This will help you to avoid having to excessively refill the feeder.

FEEDER PLACEMENT

Hanging the feeder in a place that gives both you and the hummingbirds easy access is advisable. Bird enthusiasts recommend hanging a feeder at a height of between 4 and about 8 feet. At this height, the feeder will not be so low as to prevent hummingbirds from comfortably accessing it. A feeder that is too low may also be more likely to attract wildlife other than hummingbirds. Raccoons, squirrels, or other animals may be able to feed from a feeder that is too low to the ground. Bird-watchers have also noted that putting up a feeder on a window, or placing a hanging feeder near a large window, can cause hummingbirds to fly into the window and die or be injured. Even though a window feeder may seem like the most convenient way to observe hummingbirds, it may not be the safest.

You can also take measures to maximize the number of hummingbirds that will visit your feeder. If you put up one feeder, there is the potential that one hummingbird will be able to include the feeder as part of its territory and prevent other hummingbirds from accessing it. If this appears to be happening, you might try hanging another feeder at another location and distance from the ground. If the two feeders are separated from each other by enough distance, no one hummingbird will be as likely to be able to chase all the other hummingbirds from your feeders. You might also try to put the

Taking Down the Feeder

A hummingbird that is in its normal breeding range and is visiting a feeder will generally not delay its migration because you keep a feeder up into the fall. Scientists have noted that taking down a feeder can actually hurt the chances of survival for hummingbirds that have been visiting it, given that the birds may need to use the nectar to gain weight and prepare for migration. The decision to take a feeder down may also harm any hummingbirds that are outside of their normal breeding ranges and have been visiting the feeder. A rufous hummingbird, for example, that has been visiting a feeder in the eastern United States can already be considered a migratory "vagrant," a bird that has not followed the usual migratory routes. In this context, the hummingbird may not migrate south at all and may suffer as a result of the absence of the feeder. Rufous hummingbirds that winter in parts of the United States often appear to be very dependent on feeders for survival.

Researchers have noted that the amount of naturally available nectar is unlikely to be a factor that determines the timing of a hummingbird's migration. Migration is mainly thought to be driven by increases or decreases in the amount of daylight and other seasonal factors. Thus if the desire to keep a feeder up is there, the decision to take it down should probably be based on the occurrence of a consistently low air temperature, one that would freeze the sugar solution, and not on "second-guessing" the wisdom of a hummingbird that is visiting the feeder.

feeder in a location that shields it as much as possible from strong winds and direct sunlight.

Although insects are probably the major potential nuisance you might have to deal with, it may also be advisable to prepare for visits by other birds and mammals. Bats, for example, reportedly visit hummingbird feeders in some locations. Some species of bats are nectar feeders, even though they do not feed as exclusively on nectar as do hummingbirds. If you live in the southern or southwestern states and have a hummingbird feeder, it makes sense to thus take measures to prevent bats from entering your home. This is likely to be especially important if your hummingbird feeder is on a patio. Other types of birds, especially orioles, may feed from a hummingbird feeder. If this becomes undesirable for you, it is possible to buy a feeder designed only for orioles. Although orioles, cardinals, and other types of birds, including woodpeckers, may visit a hummingbird feeder, this is not necessarily undesirable.

Making the Artificial Nectar Solution

The plants that hummingbirds pollinate produce nectar that contains in the sugar portion about 99 percent sucrose, and researchers have found that hummingbirds prefer sucrose over other sugars. Under experimental conditions, hummingbirds prefer sucrose-containing nectar over nectar that contains glucose and fructose, alone or mixed together. Sucrose is the sugar that is found in commercial sugars sold in grocery stores. Researchers think that young hummingbirds imprint on sucrose. Hummingbirds' preference for sucrose over fructose in particular thus appears to be more about taste or "familiarity" produced by imprinting at a young age than about the digestibility of sucrose. Sucrose solutions are not processed by the birds' digestive tracts any more quickly than glucose itself. Sucrose is broken down into glucose and fructose in the digestive tract, but the glucose liberated from this digestion appears to be especially important metabolically. Although

At the right time of year, a full backyard feeder can cause a feeding frenzy as hummingbirds jostle each other for a sip of artificial nectar.

Neophobia and the Willingness to Use Feeders

Researchers use the term neophobic to describe animals that do not readily eat from new types or sources of food. In the context of hummingbird research, new food options typically take the form of artificial feeders created by humans. Three species of North American hummingbirds—rufous, broad-tailed, and ruby-throated—readily adapt to and use artificial feeders. Part of this willingness stems from the ease with which these hummingbirds can learn by observation as well as from other hummingbirds in social situations. In contrast, a number of hummingbird species that live full-time at tropical latitudes are known to not be very willing to immediately begin using artificial feeders. Researchers also think that the long migrations of North American hummingbirds may require them to adapt to a wide variety of new habitats, both from year to year and at different points along their migration journeys. In contrast, tropical hummingbirds may not have to move through as many different habitats.

hummingbirds prefer sucrose over glucose in nectars, the birds' preference for glucose over the least-favored choice—fructose by itself—is especially significant. There may be a metabolic component, perhaps in addition to a taste distinction, to the dislike that hummingbirds have toward fructose. This is because fructose elevates blood glucose very slowly and can be rapidly converted into triglycerides, or fats, in the liver.

To make an artificial nectar solution, researchers and bird enthusiasts recommend using a 4:1 ratio, by volume, of water to granulated white sugar. To make this solution, you could add ½ cup of sugar to 2 cups of water. It is advisable not to substitute other kinds of sugar for the granulated white variety because the crystals of other types of sugar have different densities. It is also recommended that you boil the sugar and water for two minutes. This will sterilize the water and sugar and will also help dissolve the sucrose. Allow the solution to cool down before you pour it into the feeder.

Using Plants to Attract Hummingbirds to Feeders

Hummingbirds may be more attracted to a feeder placed in the vicinity of flowering plants that are pollinated by hummingbirds. Two general categories of plants that hummingbirds visit are perennials and annuals. Perennial plants are those that survive the winter in the ground and flower for multiple years. Annual plants, in contrast, die after flowering. You thus have to replant the seeds for annual plants each year. Annual plants may, however, flower for more prolonged periods of time in their one year of life than do perennials. Another category, which may or may not be viewed separately, consists of the various flowering vines whose nectar hummingbirds will eat. The list of flowering plants that hummingbirds will feed from is very long, but what follows is a number of well-known plants that you might want to plant, perhaps near a feeder, in a garden.

Some perennial plants that hummingbirds visit are dahlias, geraniums, penstemons, columbines, coral bells, fuchsias, cardinal flowers, century plants (a type of agave plant), delphiniums, aloes, bee balms, culinary sages and other sages within the genus *Salvia*, gladiolas, hollyhocks, and hibiscuses. One perennial vine that hummingbirds feed from is the trumpet honeysuckle.

Some annuals that hummingbirds feed from are begonias, flowering tobaccos, geraniums, impatiens, nasturtiums, petunias, pineapple sages, scarlet sages, Texas sages, and zinnias. An annual vine that hummingbirds eat nectar from is the hyacinth bean vine. One annual plant that ruby-throated hummingbirds are known to visit is the jewelweed, or spotted jewelweed (*Impatiens capensis* and other species). Although it is not possible to say that jewelweed is a "favorite" of ruby-throated hummingbirds, there is evidence that this species eats jewelweed nectar often before beginning the fall migration.

Resources

BOOKS

Burton, Robert. *The World of the Hummingbird.* Buffalo, NY: Firefly Books, 2001.

This detailed and well-researched book contains sections about many aspects of hummingbird behavior. The author includes a mixture of information about tropical and North American hummingbirds.

Greenewalt, Crawford H. *Hummingbirds.* New York, NY: Dover Publications, 1991.

Originally published in 1960, this book contains in-depth information about the flight movements and iridescent coloration of hummingbirds. Greenewalt was a hummingbird researcher who published numerous articles on hummingbirds in scientific journals. For anyone who wants in-depth, technical information on hummingbird flight as well as on early methods for photographing hummingbirds, this book is authoritative and still cited by researchers in the scientific literature.

Holloway, Joel E., and George Miksch Sutton. *Dictionary of Birds of the United States: Scientific and Common Names.* Portland, OR: Timber Press, Inc., 2003.

Includes details on the Latin and Greek words from which the names of many species of hummingbirds have been derived.

Long, Kim. *Hummingbirds: A Wildlife Handbook.* Boulder, CO: Johnson Books, 1997.

Additional information on the name derivations of various species of hummingbirds.

Sayre, Jeff, and April Pulley Sayre. *Hummingbirds: The Sun Catchers.* Minneapolis, MN: NorthWord Press, 1996.

Contains an excellent discussion of the behaviors and nesting approaches of hummingbirds and the ways in which hummingbirds interact with different flowers. The authors also include a concise species guide and information about setting up feeders.

Stokes, Donald, and Lillian Stokes. *Stokes Hummingbird Book: The Complete Guide to Attracting, Identifying, and Enjoying Hummingbirds.* New York, NY: Little, Brown and Company, 1989.

As a good overview of the behaviors and biology of hummingbirds, this book gives the reader a good sense for some of the characteristics that make each North American species unique.

Thurston, Harry. *The World of the Hummingbird.* San Francisco, CA: Sierra Club Books, 1999.

In this very readable and well-researched book, the author discusses some of the terminology that has been used to describe hummingbirds' behavior. This approach introduces the reader to some of the specifics in the research.

True, Dan. *Hummingbirds of North America: Attracting, Feeding, and Photographing.* Albuquerque, NM: University of New Mexico Press, 1994.

Mixes discussions of research with the author's firsthand observations of hummingbirds. Details about each species can serve as a stand-alone resource or a jumping-off point for readers who want to investigate further. The author also discusses some of his own experiences with photographing hummingbirds.

Williamson, Sheri. *Attracting and Feeding Hummingbirds.* Neptune City, NJ: T.F.H. Publications, 2000.

Williamson is well known as an expert on hummingbirds. This book provides useful information about plants that hummingbirds visit and about strategies for setting up feeders. Includes a compact species guide.

———. *A Field Guide to Hummingbirds of North America.* New York, NY: Houghton Mifflin, 2002.

This scholarly book provides in-depth information on North American species, including species that do not routinely breed in the United States but live primarily in Mexico. The well-referenced species data allow the reader to learn about any individual species in more detail in the journals. The book also includes information about name derivations and about the distinctive characteristics of different hummingbird genera.

WATCHING AND ATTRACTING

Birding.com

www.birding.com

This site contains links to all the various websites related to bird-watching in each state. The site also contains links to audio recordings of hummingbird sounds.

Hummingbirds.net

www.hummingbirds.net

Includes links to events related to the watching or banding of hummingbirds.

Hummingbird World

www.hummingbirdworld.com

Includes information and tips about attracting hummingbirds and also has external links for ordering many different types of hummingbird feeders.

Humnet

http://www.museum.lsu.edu/~Remsen/HUMNETintro.html

Instructions on joining an e-mail forum run by scientists at Louisiana State University that allows people to exchange information about attracting and viewing hummingbirds in the southeastern states. The messages about hummingbirds that people exchange in the forum range from very scientific to humorous.

Southeastern Arizona Bird Observatory (SABO)

www.sabo.org

The website of SABO, a nonprofit research organization that bands hummingbirds and promotes the conservation of different species of birds. Has information about banding events and about places in the United States that have large populations and diversities of hummingbirds.

HOT SPOTS AND EVENTS

Arizona–Sonora Desert Museum

http://www.desertmuseum.org/

This museum has members of some hummingbird species in captivity. It also has feeders outside that attract various species of hummingbirds.

Big Bend National Park

http://www.nps.gov/bibe/

One of the sites where a number of species of hummingbirds breed in the summer. These species include blue-throated, lucifer, and white-eared hummingbirds. Much research on these and other species of hummingbirds has been done in this area of Texas. The park is 70 to 100 miles from any town of significant size. If you visit the park, it is advisable to make sure your cell phone works in case of an emergency.

Cave Creek Ranch

http://cavecreekranch.com/

A small lodging area in Arizona's Chiricahua Mountains and a popular destination for both hummingbird researchers and enthusiasts for more than thirty years. At least fourteen species of hummingbirds can be seen here at different times, especially in the summer and early fall.

Hummer / Bird Celebration

http://www.rockporthummingbird.com/

This is an event that takes place in Rockport and Fulton, two small towns along the Gulf coast in Texas, for four days each September. It includes educational and informative talks given by experts, banding events, and organized birding excursions. The festival was originally set up to coincide with the fall migration of ruby-throated hummingbirds but has since expanded to include other aspects of birding.

Hummer / Bird Study Group
www.hummingbirdsplus.org

> Bob and Martha Sargent set up this nonprofit organization to do banding research on hummingbirds and work related to the conservation of hummingbird habitats. The group has a banding station and carries out banding events at Fort Morgan State Historical Park in Alabama. Anyone can visit these events. Members of the group have banded many ruby-throated hummingbirds and other birds that are trans-Gulf migrants.

Madera Canyon
http://www.fs.fed.us/r3/coronado/forest/recreation/camping/sites/madera.shtml

> People visiting the canyon may be able to see various species of hummingbirds on the hiking trails, and some of the lodging sites have hummingbird feeders.

Patagonia–Sonoita Creek Preserve
http://www.nature.org/wherewework/northamerica/states/arizona/
preserves/art1972.html

> Numerous species of hummingbirds are likely to be living in the area, and the Nature Conservancy offers nature walks that may interest birders.

Ramsey Canyon Preserve
http://www.nature.org/wherewework/northamerica/states/arizona/
preserves/art1973.html

> Visitors can potentially see any of up to fourteen species of hummingbirds.

Southwest Wings Birding and Nature Festival
http://www.swwings.org/

> This festival takes place in August, in Sierra Vista, Arizona, and is run by a nonprofit organization.

VOLUNTEERING OPPORTUNITIES
Birchside Studios
www.birchsidestudios.com

> This site has contact information for people who want to participate in banding research, directed by scientists working through the Hummingbird Monitoring Network, on hummingbirds at Madera Canyon, in Arizona. The site also includes information about birding in different states.

Hummingbird Banding Program
http://members.cox.net/ldavis610/

> Allows you to contact researchers associated with the Hummingbird Monitoring Network if you want to participate in banding research at Fort Huachuca.

Hummingbird Monitoring Network
www.hummonnet.org

> This organization provides opportunities for hummingbird enthusiasts to volunteer and participate in banding research. Researchers carry out these banding events at Fort Huachuca and at Madera Canyon.

SABO Banding Events and Volunteer Opportunities
http://www.sabo.org/photoalb/banding.htm

SABO allows volunteers to do various tasks and holds banding events at this station. One volunteer recently started an "Adopt a Hummingbird" program, discussed on this site, that provides people with pictures and banding numbers for individual hummingbirds.

HUMMINGBIRDS IN MYTHOLOGY

Birdwell, D. B. Review: *The Making of Modern Belize: Politics, Society, and British Colonialism in Central America* by C. H. Grant. *American Journal of Sociology* 84, no. 3 (1978): 781–83.

Fash, W. L. "Changing Perspectives on Maya Civilization." *Annual Review of Anthropology* 23 (1994): 181–208.

Hellbom, A. B. "Man-like Gods and Deified Men in Mexican Cosmolore." *Folklore* 10 (1999): 7–56.

Levi, J. M. "Myth and History Reconsidered: Archaeological Implications of Tzotzil-Maya Mythology." *American Antiquity* 53, no. 3 (1988): 605–19.

Urban, G. "Agent- and Patient-Centricity in Myth." *Journal of American Folklore* 94, no. 373 (1981): 323–44.

———. "Speech about Speech in Speech about Action." *Journal of American Folklore* 97, no. 385 (1984): 310–28.

Vogt, E. Review: *The Transformation of the Hummingbird: Cultural Roots of a Zinacantecan Mythical Poem* by Eva Hunt. *American Anthropologist, New Series* 1978; 80(4): 964–965.

Witzel, Michael. "Vala and Iwato: The Myth of the Hidden Sun in India, Japan, and Beyond." *Electronic Journal of Vedic Studies* 2005; 12(1): 1-69.

JOURNAL ARTICLES
Territorial Interactions, Nesting Territories, Breeding Territories, and Traplining

Altshuler, D. L. "Flight Performance and Competitive Displacement of Hummingbirds across Elevational Gradients." *American Naturalist* 167, no. 2 (2006): 216–29.

Altshuler, D. L., and R. Dudley. "The Ecological and Evolutionary Interface of Hummingbird Flight Physiology." *Journal of Experimental Biology* 205, no. 16 (2002): 2325–36.

Altshuler, D. L. et al. "Of Hummingbirds and Helicopters: Hovering Costs, Competitive Ability, and Foraging Strategies." *American Naturalist* 163, no. 1 (2004): 16–25.

Atwood, J. L. et al. "Temporal Patterns of Singing Activity at Leks of the White-bellied Emerald." *Wilson Bulletin* 103, no. 3 (1991): 373–386.

Avery, M. L., and C. van Riper III. "Post-Breeding Territoriality and Foraging Behavior in Costa's Hummingbird (*Calypte costae*)." *Southwestern Naturalist* 38, no. 4 (1993): 374–77.

Baum, K. A., and W. E. Grant. "Hummingbird Foraging Behavior in Different Patch Types: Simulation of Alternative Strategies." *Ecological Modelling* 137, no. 2 (2001): 201–9.

Bleiweiss, R. "Origin of Hummingbird Faunas." *Biological Journal of the Linnean Society* 65, no. 1 (1998): 77–97.

———. "Phylogeny, Body Mass, and Genetic Consequences of Lek-Mating Behavior in Hummingbirds." *Molecular Biology and Evolution* 15, no. 5 (1998): 492–98.

Boyden, T. C. "Territorial Defense against Hummingbirds and Insects by Tropical Hummingbirds." *Condor* 80, no. 2 (1978): 216–21.

Brown, J. H., and M. A. Bowers. "Community Organization in Hummingbirds: Relationships Between Morphology and Ecology." *Auk* 102, no. 2 (1985): 251–69.

Brown, J. H., and A. Kodric-Brown. "Convergence, Competition, and Mimicry in a Temperate Community of Hummingbird-Pollinated Flowers." *Ecology* 60, no. 5 (1979): 1022–35.

Carpenter, F. L. "Food Abundance and Territoriality: To Defend or Not to Defend?" *American Zoologist* 27, no. 2 (1987): 387–99.

Carpenter, F. L. et al. "Interference Asymmetries among Age-Sex Classes of Rufous Hummingbirds during Migratory Stopovers." *Behavioral Ecology and Sociobiology* 33, no. 5 (1993): 297–304.

Ewald, P. W., and S. Rohwer. "Age, Coloration, and Dominance in Nonbreeding Hummingbirds: A Test of the Asymmetry Hypothesis." *Behavioral Ecology and Sociobiology* 7, no. 4 (1980): 273–79.

Feinsinger, P. "Organization of a Tropical Guild of Nectarivorous Birds." *Ecological Monographs* 46, no. 3 (1976): 257–91.

Feinsinger, P., and S. B. Chaplin. "On the Relationship between Wing Disc Loading and Foraging Strategy in Hummingbirds." *American Naturalist* 109, no. 966 (1975): 217–24.

Feinsinger, P., and R. K. Colwell. "Community Organization among Neotropical Nectar-Feeding Birds." *American Zoologist* 18, no. 4 (1978): 779–95.

Ferreira, A. R. J. et al. "Vocalizations and Associated Behaviors of the Sombre Hummingbird (*Aphantochroa cirrhochloris*) and the Rufous-breasted Hermit (*Glaucis hirsutus*)." *Auk* 123, no. 4 (2006): 1129–48.

Ficken, M. S. et al. "Reproductive Behavior and Communication in Blue-Throated Hummingbirds." *Wilson Bulletin* 114, no. 2 (2002): 197–209.

Garrison, J. S. E., and C. L. Gass. "Response of a Traplining Hummingbird to Changes in Nectar Availability." *Behavioral Ecology* 10, no. 6 (1999): 714–25.

Gass, C. L., and J. S. E. Garrison. "Energy Regulation by Traplining Hummingbirds." *Functional Ecology* 13, no. 4 (1999): 483–92.

Giraldeau, L. A., and R. Ydenberg. "The Center-edge Effect: The Result of a War of Attrition between Territorial Contestants?" *Auk* 104, no. 3 (1987): 535–38.

Hernandez, H. M., and V. M. Toledo. "The Role of Nectar Robbers and Pollinators in the Reproduction of *Erythrina leptorhiza*." *Annals of the Missouri Botanical Garden* 66, no. 3 (1979): 512–20.

Kodric-Brown, A., and J. H. Brown. "Influence of Economics, Interspecific Competition, and Sexual Dimorphism on Territoriality of Migrant Rufous Hummingbirds." *Ecology* 59, no. 2 (1978): 285–96.

Kuban, J. F., and R. L. Neill. "Feeding Ecology of Hummingbirds in the Highlands of the Chisos Mountains, Texas." *Condor* 82, no. 2 (1980): 180–85.

Neill, D. A. "Trapliners in the Trees: Hummingbird Pollination of *Erythrina*; Sect. *Erythrina* (Leguminosae: Papolionoideae)." *Annals of the Missouri Botanical Garden* 74, no. 1 (1987): 27–41.

Paton, D. C., and F. L. Carpenter. "Peripheral Foraging by Territorial Rufous Hummingbirds: Defense by Exploitation." *Ecology* 65, no. 6 (1984): 1808–19.

Pitelka, F. A. "Territoriality and Related Problems in North American Humming-birds." *Condor* 44, no. 5 (1942): 189–204.

Powers, D. R., and T. McKee. "The Effect of Food Availability on Time and Energy Expenditures of Territorial and Non-Territorial Hummingbirds." *Condor* 96, no. 4 (1994): 1064–75.

Sandlin, E. A. "Cue Use Affects Resource Subdivision among Three Coexisting Hum-mingbird Species." *Behavioral Ecology* 11, no. 5 (2000): 550–59.

Stiles, G. F., and L. L. Wold. "Ecology and Evolution of Lek Mating Behavior in the Long-tailed Hermit Hummingbird." *Ornithological Monographs* 27 (1979): 1–78.

Tamm, S. et al. "Display Behavior of Male Calliope Hummingbirds during the Breed-ing Season." *Condor* 91, no. 2 (1989): 272–79.

Tamm, S. "Breeding Territory Quality and Agonistic Behavior: Effects of Energy Availability and Intruder Pressure in Hummingbirds." *Behavioral Ecology and Sociobiology* 16, no. 3 (1985): 203–7.

———. "Importance of Energy Costs in Central Place Foraging by Hummingbirds." *Ecology* 70, no. 1 (1989): 195–205.

Temeles, E. J. "Reversed Sexual Size Dimorphism: Effect on Resource Defense and Foraging Behaviors of Nonbreeding Northern Harriers." *Auk* 103, no. 1 (1986): 70–78.

Tiebout, H. M. III. "Costs and Benefits of Interspecific Dominance Rank: Are Subordi-nates Better at Finding Novel Food Locations?" *Animal Behavior* 51, no. 6 (1996): 1375–81.

———. "Mechanisms of Competition in Tropical Hummingbirds: Metabolic Costs for Losers and Winners." *Ecology* 74, no. 2 (1993): 405–18.

Valdivia, C. E., and P. L. Gonzales-Gomez. "A Trade-Off between the Amount and Distance of Pollen Dispersal Triggered by the Mixed Foraging Behaviour of *Sephanoides sephaniodes* (Trochilidae) on *Lapageria rosea* (Philesiaceae)." *Acta Oeco-logica* 29, no. 3 (2006): 324–27.

Wikelski, M. et al. "Reproductive Seasonality of Seven Neotropical Passerine Species." *Condor* 105, no. 4 (2003): 683–95.

Wolf, L. L. "Female Territoriality in the Purple-Throated Carib." *Auk* 92, no. 3 (1975): 511–22.

Anatomy, Physiology, Feeding, Memory, and Flight

Aldrich, E. C. "Pterylography and Molt of the Allen Hummingbird." *Condor* 58, no. 2 (1956): 121–33.

Altshuler, D. L., and R. Dudley. "Kinematics of Hovering Hummingbird Flight along Simulated and Natural Elevational Gradients." *Journal of Experimental Biology* 206, no. 18 (2003): 3139–47.

Altshuler, D. L. et al. "Resolution of a Paradox: Hummingbird Flight at High Eleva-tion Does Not Come Without a Cost." *Proceedings of the National Academy of Sci-ences of the United States of America* 101, no. 51 (2004): 17,731–36.

Bakken, B. H. et al. "Hummingbirds Arrest Their Kidneys at Night: Diel Variation in Glomerular Filtration Rate in *Selasphorus Platycercus*." *Journal of Experimental Biol-ogy* 207, no. 25 (2004): 4383–91.

Baltosser, W. H. "Annual Molt in Ruby-Throated and Black-Chinned Humming-birds." *Condor* 97, no. 2 (1995): 484–91.

Beuchat, C. A., and C. R. Chong. "Hyperglycemia in Hummingbirds and Its Consequences for Hemoglobin Glycation." *Comparative Biochemistry and Physiology: Part A* 120, no. 3 (1998): 409–16.

Bleiweiss, R. "Iridescent Polychromatism in a Female Hummingbird: Is It Related to Feeding Strategies?" *Auk* 102, no. 4 (1985): 701–13.

Bock, W. J. "Organisms as Functional Machines: A Connectivity Explanation." *American Zoologist* 29, no. 3 (1989): 1119–32.

Brown, J. H., and M. A. Bowers. "Community Organization in Hummingbirds: Relationships between Morphology and Ecology." *Auk* 102, no. 2 (1985): 251–69.

Brown, J. H. "Correlates and Consequences of Body Size in Nectar-Feeding Birds." *American Zoologist* 18, no. 4 (1978): 687–700.

Carpenter, F. L. et al. "Why Hummingbirds Have Such Large Crops." *Evolutionary Ecology* 5, no. 4 (1991): 405–14.

Chai, P., and D. Millard. "Flight and Size Constraints: Hovering Performance of Large Hummingbirds under Maximal Loading." *Journal of Experimental Biology* 200, no. 21 (1997): 2757–63.

DeBenedictis, P. A. et al. "Optimal Meal Size in Hummingbirds." *American Naturalist* 112, no. 984 (1978): 301–16.

Eduardo, J. et al. "Locomotion and Thermogenesis in Hummingbirds." *Comparative Biochemistry and Physiology: Part B* 120, no. 1 (1998): 27–33.

Ewald, P. W., and W. A. Williams. "Function of the Bill and Tongue in Nectar Uptake by Hummingbirds." *Auk* 99, no. 3 (1982): 573–76.

Gass, C. L., and W. M. Roberts. "The Problem of Temporal Scale in Optimization: Three Contrasting Views of Hummingbird Visits to Flowers." *American Naturalist* 140, no. 5 (1992): 829–53.

Greenewalt, C. H. et al. "The Iridescent Colors of Hummingbird Feathers." *Proceedings of the American Philosophical Society* 104, no. 3 (1960): 249–53.

Hainsworth, F. R. "On the Tongue of a Hummingbird: Its Role in the Rate and Energetics of Feeding." *Comparative Biochemistry and Physiology: Part A* 46, no. 1 (1973): 65–78.

Healy, S., and T. A. Hurly. "Hummingbirds." *Current Biology* 16, no. 11 (2006): R392–93.

Henderson, J. et al. "Rufous Hummingbirds' Memory for Flower Location." *Animal Behavior* 61, no. 5 (2001): 981–86.

———. "Timing in Free-Living Rufous Hummingbirds: *Selasphorus rufus*." *Current Biology* 16, no. 5 (2006): 512–15.

Hiebert, S. "Seasonal Changes in Body Mass and Use of Torpor in a Migratory Hummingbird." *Auk* 110, no. 4 (1993): 787–97.

Hiebert, S. M. "Time-Dependent Thresholds for Torpor Initiation in the Rufous Hummingbird (*Selasphorus rufus*)." *Journal of Comparative Physiology B* 162, no. 3 (1992): 249–55.

Hiebert, S. M. et al. "Corticosterone and Nocturnal Torpor in the Rufous Hummingbird (*Selasphorus rufus*)." *General and Comparative Endocrinology* 120, no. 2 (2000): 220–34.

Hurly, T. A. "Spatial Memory in Rufous Hummingbirds: Memory for Rewarded and Non-Rewarded Sites." *Animal Behavior* 51, no. 1 (1996): 177–83.

Hurly, T. A., and S. D. Healy. "Memory for Flowers in Rufous Hummingbirds: Location or Local Visual Cues?" *Animal Behavior* 51, no. 5 (1996): 1149–57.

Iwaniuk, A. N., and D. R. W. Wylie. "Neural Specialization for Hovering in Hummingbirds: Hypertrophy of the Pretectal Nucleus Lentiformis Mesencephali." *Journal of Comparative Neurology* 500, no. 2 (2007): 211–21.

Karasov, W. H. et al. "Food Passage and Intestinal Nutrient Absorption in Hummingbirds." *Auk* 103, no. 3 (1986): 453–64.

Larimer, J. L., and R. Dudley. "Accelerational Implications of Hummingbird Display Dives." *Auk* 112, no. 4 (1995): 1064–66.

Lasiewski, R. C., and R. J. Lasiewski. "Physiological Responses of the Blue-throated and Rivoli's Hummingbirds." *Auk* 84, no. 1 (1967): 34–48.

Lindstedt, S. L. et al. "Task-Specific Design of Skeletal Muscle: Balancing Muscle Structural Composition." *Comparative Biochemistry and Physiology: Part B* 120, no. 1 (1998): 35–40.

Lopez-Calleja, M. V. et al. "Effects of Sugar Concentration on Hummingbird Feeding and Energy Use." *Comparative Biochemistry and Physiology: Part A* 118, no. 4 (1997): 1291–99.

Martinez del Rio, C. "Sugar Preferences in Hummingbirds: The Influence of Subtle Chemical Differences on Food Choice." *Condor* 92, no. 4 (1990): 1022–30.

McWhorter, T. J., and C. Martinez del Rio. "Food Ingestion and Water Turnover in Hummingbirds: How Much Dietary Water Is Absorbed?" *Journal of Experimental Biology* 202, no. 20 (1999): 2851–58.

Odum, E. P. et al. "Flight Energy and Estimated Flight Ranges of Some Migratory Birds." *Auk* 78, no. 4 (1961): 515–27.

Osorio, D., and A. D. Ham. "Spectral Reflectance and Directional Properties of Structural Coloration in Bird Plumage." *Journal of Experimental Biology* 205, no. 14 (2002): 2017–27.

Roberts, W. M. "Hummingbird Licking Behavior and the Energetics of Nectar Feeding." *Auk* 112, no. 2 (1995): 456–63.

———. "Hummingbirds' Nectar Concentration Preferences at Low Volume: The Importance of Time Scale." *Animal Behavior* 52, no. 2 (1996): 361–70.

Schmidt-Lebuhn, A. N. et al. "Hummingbirds as Drivers of Plant Speciation?" *Trends in Plant Science* 12, no. 8 (2007): 329–31.

Shawkey, M. D., and G. E. Hill. "Significance of a Basal Melanin Layer to Production of Non-Iridescent Structural Plumage Color: Evidence from an Amelanotic Steller's Jay (*Cyanocitta stelleri*)." *Journal of Experimental Biology* 209, no. 7 (2006): 1245–50.

Staron, R. S. Human "Skeletal Muscle Fiber Type Adaptability to Various Workloads." *Journal of Histochemistry and Cytochemistry* 32, no. 2 (1984): 146–52.

Stettenheim, P. R. "The Integumentary Morphology of Modern Birds: An Overview." *American Zoologist* 40, no. 4 (2000): 461–77.

Stiles, G. F. "Behavioral, Ecological, and Morphological Correlates of Foraging for Arthropods by the Hummingbirds of a Tropical Wet Forest." *Condor* 97, no. 4 (1995): 853–78.

———. "Intraspecific and Interspecific Variation in Molt Patterns of Some Tropical Hummingbirds." *Auk* 112, no. 1 (1995): 118–32.

Suarez, R. K. "Hummingbird Flight: Sustaining the Highest Mass-specific Metabolic Rates among Vertebrates." *Cellular and Molecular Life Sciences* 48, no. 6 (1992): 565–70.

———. "Mitochondrial Respiration in Hummingbird Flight Muscles." *Proceedings of the National Academy of Sciences of the United States of America* 88, no. 11 (1991): 4870–73.

Suarez, R. K., and C. L. Gass. "Hummingbird Foraging and the Relation Between Bioenergetics and Behaviour." *Comparative Biochemistry and Physiology: Part A* 133, no. 2 (2002): 335–43.

Suarez, R. K. et al. Abstract: "Breakfast of Champions; Energetics of Hummingbird Foraging at Low Ambient Temperature." *Comparative Biochemistry and Physiology: Part A* 124, suppl. 1 (1999): S64.

Temeles, E. J. "A New Dimension to Hummingbird-Flower Relationships." *Oecologia* 105, no. 4 (1996): 517–23.

Tobalske, B. W. et al. "Three-Dimensional Kinematics of Hummingbird Flight." *Journal of Experimental Biology* 210, no. 13 (2007): 2368–82.

Welch, K. C., Jr. et al. "Oxygen Consumption Rates in Hovering Hummingbirds Reflect Substrate-Dependent Differences in P/O Ratios: Carbohydrate as a 'Premium Fuel.'" *Journal of Experimental Biology* 210, no. 12 (2007): 2146–53.

Williamson, F. S. L. "The Molt and Testis Cycles of the Anna Hummingbird." *Condor* 58, no. 5 (1956): 342–66.

Wylie, D. R. W., and N. A. Crowder. "Spatiotemporal Properties of Fast and Slow Neurons in the Pretectal Nucleus Lentiformis Mesencephali in Pigeons." *Journal of Neurophysiology* 84, no. 5 (2000): 2529–40.

Yoshioka, S., and S. Kinoshita. "Effect of Macroscopic Structure in Iridescent Color of the Peacock Feather." *Forma* 17, no. 2 (2002): 169–81.

Nesting, Development, Flight Displays, Predation, and Other Topics

Altmann, S. A. "Avian Mobbing Behavior and Predator Recognition." *Condor* 58, no. 4 (1956): 241–53.

Altshuler, D. L., and A. M. Nunn. "Observational Learning in Hummingbirds." *Auk* 118, no. 3 (2001): 795–99.

Astheimer, L. B. "Long Laying Intervals: A Possible Mechanism and Its Implications." *Auk* 102, no. 2 (1985): 401–9.

Baltosser, W. H. "Nectar Availability and Habitat Selection by Hummingbirds in Guadalupe Canyon." *Wilson Bulletin* 101, no. 4 (1989): 559–78.

———. "Nesting Success and Productivity of Hummingbirds in Southwestern New Mexico and Southeastern Arizona." *Wilson Bulletin* 93, no. 3 (1986): 353–67.

Bene, F. "The Role of Learning in the Feeding Behavior of Black-Chinned Hummingbirds." *Condor* 47, no. 1 (1945): 3–22.

Calder, W. A. "Microhabitat Selection during Nesting of Hummingbirds in the Rocky Mountains." *Ecology* 54, no. 1 (1973): 127–34.

———. "Temperature Relationships and Nesting of the Calliope Hummingbird." *Condor* 73, no. 3 (1971): 314–21.

Carpenter, F. L., and J. L. Castronova. "Maternal Diet Selectivity in Calypte Anna." *American Midland Naturalist* 103, no. 1 (1980): 175–79.

Constantz, G. D. "Growth of Nestling Rufous Hummingbirds." *Auk* 97, no. 3 (1980): 622–24.

Elliston, E. P., and W. H. Baltosser. "Sex Ratios and Bill Growth in Nestling Black-Chinned Hummingbirds." *Western Birds* 26, no. 2 (1995): 76–81.

Ficken, M. S. "Parent-Offspring Conflict in Blue-Throated Hummingbirds." *Southwestern Naturalist* 47, no. 1 (2002): 118–21.

Finley, W. L. "Hummingbird Studies." *Condor* 7, no. 3 (1905): 59–62.

Gamboa, G. J. "Predation on Rufous Hummingbird by Wied's Crested Flycatcher." *Auk* 94, no. 1 (1977): 157–58.

Garcia-C., J. M., and R. A. Zahawi. "Predation by a Blue-Crowned Motmot (*Momotus momota*) on a Hummingbird." *Wilson Journal of Ornithology* 118, no. 2 (2006): 261–63.

Graves, G. R. "Predation on Hummingbird by Oropendola." *Condor* 80, no. 2 (1978): 251.

Hixon, M. A., and F. L. Carpenter. "Distinguishing Energy Maximizers from Time Minimizers: A Comparative Study of Two Hummingbird Species." *American Zoologist* 28, no. 3 (1988): 913–25.

Kelly, J. W. "History of the Nesting of an Anna Hummingbird." *Condor* 57, no. 6 (1955): 347–53.

Lara, C., and J. F. Ornelas. "Preferential Nectar Robbing of Flowers with Long Corollas: Experimental Studies of Two Hummingbird Species Visiting Three Plant Species." *Oecologia* 128, no. 2 (2001): 263–73.

Laverty, T. M., and R. C. Plowright. "Competition between Hummingbirds and Bumble Bees for Nectar in Flowers of *Impatiens biflora*." *Oecologia* 66, no. 1 (1985): 25–32.

Lima, S. L. "Energy, Predators and the Behaviour of Feeding Hummingbirds." *Evolutionary Ecology* 5, no. 3 (1991): 220–30.

Marin, M. "Postnatal Development of the Violet Sabrewing in Costa Rica." *Wilson Bulletin* 113, no. 1 (2001): 110–14.

Miller, R. S., and C. L. Gass. "Survivorship in Hummingbirds: Is Predation Important?" *Auk* 102, no. 1 (1985): 175–78.

Montgomerie, R. D., and C. A. Redsell. "A Nesting Hummingbird Feeding Solely on Arthropods." *Condor* 82, no. 4 (1980): 463–64.

Oniki, Y., and E. O. Willis. "Nesting Behavior of the Swallow-Tailed Hummingbird, *Eupetomena macroura* (Trochilidae, Aves)." *Brazilian Journal of Biology* 60, no. 4 (2000): 655–62.

Ornelas, J. F. "Serrate Tomia: An Adaptation for Nectar Robbing in Hummingbirds?" *Auk* 111, no. 3 (1994): 703–10.

Ortiz-Crespo, F. I. "A New Method to Separate Immature and Adult Hummingbirds." *Auk* 89, no. 4 (1972): 851–57.

Owen, J. L., and J. C. Cokendolpher. "Tailless Whipscorpion (*Phrynus longipes*) Feeds on Antillean Crested Hummingbird (*Orthorhyncus cristatus*)." *Wilson Journal of Ornithology* 118, no. 3 (2006): 422–23.

Pitelka, F. A. "Breeding Seasons of Hummingbirds near Santa Barbara, California." *Condor* 53, no. 4 (1951): 198–201.

Robinson, W. D. "White-Necked Puffbird Captures Rufous-Tailed Hummingbird." *Wilson Bulletin* 115, no. 4 (2003): 486–87.

Skutch, A. F. "Life History of the Scaly-Breasted Hummingbird." *Condor* 66, no. 3 (1964): 186–98.

———. "Life History of the Violet-Headed Hummingbird." *Wilson Bulletin* 70, no. 1 (1958): 5–19.

————. "Life History of the White-Crested Coquette Hummingbird." *Wilson Bulletin* 73, no. 1 (1961): 5–10.

Stiles, G. F. "Aggressive and Courtship Displays of the Male Anna's Hummingbird." *Condor* 84, no. 2 (1982): 208–25.

————. "Possible Specialization for Hummingbird-Hunting in the Tiny Hawk." *Auk* 95, no. 3 (1978): 550–53.

Vleck, C. M. "Hummingbird Incubation: Female Attentiveness and Egg Temperature." *Oecologia* 51, no. 2 (1981): 199–205.

Waser, N. M. "Food Supply and Nest Timing of Broad-Tailed Hummingbirds in the Rocky Mountains." *Condor* 78, no. 1 (1976): 133–35.

Wolf, L. L. "'Prostitution' Behavior in a Tropical Hummingbird." *Condor* 77, no. 2 (1975): 140–44.

Wolf, L. L., and G. F. Stiles. "Evolution of Pair Cooperation in a Tropical Hummingbird." *Evolution* 24, no. 4 (1970): 759–73.

Distribution, Migration, and Conservation

Arizmendi, Maria del Coro. "Multiple Ecological Interactions: Nectar Robbers and Hummingbirds in a Highland Forest in Mexico." *Canadian Journal of Zoology* 79, no. 6 (2001): 997–1006.

Calder, W. A. III, and E. G. Jones. "Implications of Recapture Data for Migration of the Rufous Hummingbird (*Selasphorus rufus*) in the Rocky Mountains." *Auk* 106, no. 3 (1989): 488–89.

Hill, G. E. et al. "Recent Change in the Winter Distribution of Rufous Hummingbirds." *Auk* 115, no. 1 (1998): 240–45.

Phillips, A. R. "The Migrations of Allen's and Other Hummingbirds." *Condor* 77, no. 2 (1975): 196–205.

Russell, R. W. et al. "The Impact of Variation in Stopover Habitat Quality on Migrant Rufous Hummingbirds." *Conservation Biology* 8, no. 2 (1994): 483–90.

Stouffer, P. C., and R. O. Bierregaard, Jr. "Effects of Forest Fragmentation on Understory Hummingbirds in Amazonian Brazil." *Conservation Biology* 9, no. 5 (1995): 1085–94.

Tramer, E. J. "Proportions of Wintering North American Birds in Disturbed and Undisturbed Dry Tropical Habitats." *Condor* 76, no. 4 (1974): 460–64.

Wethington, S. M. et al. "Hummingbird Conservation: Discovering Diversity Patterns in Southwest U.S.A." *USDA Forest Service Proceedings* RMRS-P-36 (2005): 162–68.

Woods, R. S. "The Hummingbirds of California: Comments on Their Habits and Characteristics." *Auk* 44, no. 3 (1927): 297–318.

Index